Emergence

Journey Toward Self-Realization

Front Cover image by Author AI-assisted

By LeRoy Dingle

Disclaimer

Emergence presents a collection of essays from the Dingle Legacy Project that systematically examine my family's intergenerational experiences as a lens for exploring the construction of self-identity, resilience, and cultural continuity. The central thesis asserts that intentional engagement with familial history, through practices such as oral storytelling, collective journaling, and community participation, serves not only to preserve traditions but also to facilitate self-realization.

i

Table of Contents

Acknowledgments

Completing *these Essays on Survival, Spirit, and Self-Discovery* was a journey of the heart, history, and healing. It was possible through the efforts, encouragement, and wisdom of many who helped realize this vision.

First, I acknowledge ancestors, Cato, Selina, Sandy, Racheal, Dublin, Martha, Jessie, Sarah Jane, Isaac, Dolly Anne, and those unnamed but present. Their faith and endurance built this foundation. Every page echoes their memory and unfinished song.

Special gratitude is extended to family members who shared personal accounts, family stories, photographs, and fragments of oral history that gave shape and breath to this collection. Your memories and willingness to remember gave depth to the historical record and warmth to the words that follow. To the genealogical and historical archives, including Census data, public records, church documents, and the many researchers who preserved our history. I offer sincere thanks. Without these sources, the narrative of our people might have remained scattered and silent.

I extend my appreciation to the AI-assisted research and narrative support that organized information, interpreted patterns, and wove history with creativity. This technology served as a bridge across generations, allowing ancestral voices to resonate in new ways.

To my teachers, mentors, and colleagues, thank you for instilling discipline, service, and curiosity over 23 years in the Air Force and as a Public Administrator. Lessons of leadership, empathy, and endurance became tools for honoring this legacy.

To the Dingle descendants, near and far, who continue to live, dream, and build upon the foundation of those who came before, you are the living branches of this tree. May this book remind you that your story is sacred, your lineage is powerful, and your life is a continuation of something far greater than yourself.

Finally, I offer thanks to the Spirit of Creation itself, the source that guided each word, aligned each discovery, and carried me through moments of uncertainty. This work is a testament not only to where we come from but to who we continue to become.

Foward

Every family has a story, but not every family carries a way of seeing the world. Some families leave behind records, dates, and memories, while others leave a deeper mark, a quiet energy that resonates long after history falls silent. The Dingle family, whose journey begins in the tidal creeks of Sullivan's Island and flows through the landscapes, churches, porches, and dreams of South Carolina's Lowcountry, is one of those families that carries a unique legacy.

For over two hundred years, the Dingle experience has been shaped by significant forces that transcend individual generations: the struggles of enslavement and the triumph of emancipation, the search for faith amid doubt, the cycles of war and peace, the pull of land and migration, and the complexities of gender and spirituality. Yet, within this tapestry lies something even more profound, an evolving sense of awareness.

This book is not just a collection of stories or philosophical musings. It's a delicate weaving of ancestral memories, lived experiences, and the deep inner wisdom that has guided each generation, even when the world around them tried to erase their sense of identity.

This book delves into the emotional, spiritual, cultural, psychological, and metaphysical journeys of a people who refused to be broken. They shed light on how African cosmology has survived beneath the weight of Western teachings, how faith has transitioned from mere obedience to a more personal understanding, and how societal pressures have shaped and sometimes warped the lives of those descended from Africa. It illustrates how one family's experiences can reveal the survival strategies of an entire community.

This work documents our history and offers direction for what lies ahead. I hope that these pages provide not just insights but also a path to transformation, for my family, for all families, and for a nation still seeking a deeper understanding of itself.

With the intention of clarity and love.

Introduction

Despite my degrees and the books that shaped my mind, I never forget where I came from. I am a Southern Black man, shaped by the Lowcountry's marshlands and tidal creeks and the lessons of scarcity. My education opened doors. Yet, memories of humble beginnings, my family's quiet dignity, and my community's laughter and struggle keep me grounded. This duality, a mind tuned to learning and a heart shaped by survival, guides this work. I write and reflect from this place between worlds.

Though enslaved, my family established their lineage on Carolina soil. They resisted dehumanization and gave their descendants a sense of identity and purpose. Each generation carried forward the drive for self-determination, education, and meaning. Physical chains broke, but psychological and cultural barriers persisted.

Under the same Southern sun, I inherited my ancestors' faith and fears. My early teachings offered an external belief system. Ancestral wisdom, however, encouraged self-reflection and the discovery of authentic identity. My awakening revealed that true liberation comes from reclaiming an African-centered worldview. This view emphasizes ancestry, self-knowledge, and divine recognition within.

Freedom unfolded in stages: questioning beliefs, remembering ancestral truths, and creating a new narrative. By aligning with principles of interconnectedness, harmony, reciprocity, and self-awareness, I shifted from dependency to empowerment. This transformation allowed me to experience the universe through consciousness rather than doctrine.

Today, my journey bridges past and future generations. I strive to embody the lessons of my ancestors and the duties of an ancestor-in-training. The central lesson is clear: self-identity is shaped by what we remember, reclaim, and reimagine. Legacy is defined not only by bloodline but by evolving consciousness and commitment to self-liberation. In this continuum, I am a student and teacher, an inheritor and an architect, an echo, and a voice. These essays reflect my personal and generational journeys to self-realization and freedom.

Section one

Reality Check

In every community, the health and stability of the group are fundamentally intertwined with its social norms. These norms, which encompass shared values and customs, reflect the collective identity of the society. When individuals align with these social standards, it fosters a sense of unity and belonging, which in turn promotes the overall well-being of the community.

How I came to know Knowledge

I didn't come to know things just through textbooks, schools, or the reassuring structures of conventional beliefs. My first teachers were the tidal creeks of Sullivan's Island, South Carolina, those meandering veins of saltwater that twisted through the marshes, like ancient scribes etching tales into the silt. Long before I could articulate my thoughts, I experienced the rhythm of the tides. Before I learned the rules of doctrine, I understood the quiet language of a Lowcountry night, filled with its own kind of wisdom. And before I grasped the weight of my ancestry, I could feel it entwined in the very earth beneath my bare feet.

My understanding of the world grew not from formal education but from observation, intuition, and the whispers of generations who came before me. It wasn't something someone taught me; it was something I discovered. In time, this knowledge became the bedrock of my life, my evolution, and my writing.

Growing up near tidal waters, I learned a unique rhythm of truth. In the marshes, understanding rarely arrives all at once; it ebbs and flows. The tide instilled in me patience, humility, and the awareness that growth is a constant process. What's obscured at noon often becomes clear at dusk; what feels solid in the morning may shift by nightfall.

This ever-changing landscape laid the groundwork for how I view the world. I learned that reality has layers: a surface world for the hurried, a deeper world for those with patience, and a quiet world for those willing to listen. Even as a child, I sensed that existence isn't divided into what is known and what is unknown; instead, it's about what we are ready to perceive.

While others defined faith as a firm belief, I came to understand it as a relationship, a connection between myself, the land, the water, and a cosmic rhythm that's older than any text. Back then, I didn't have the terminology. Still, I was already embodying the principles of a faithful observer, realizing that our attention shapes our understanding, and that experience, in turn, shapes our destiny.

Long before I recognized the names of Cato, Sandy, Dublin, Jessie, Isaac, and the lineage forged through grit and dignity, I felt their presence. Growing up in the Lowcountry meant being steeped in a place where history is always close. The land remembers. The water remembers. Even the humid air carries the weight of stories.

As I grew older, I began to understand that what I had thought was mere intuition was often a deep ancestral memory, wisdom encoded through the struggle for survival. My ancestors learned to read the world without waiting for permission. They mastered the cycles of the land and seasons, the mathematics essential for survival, the spirituality woven into resilience, and the psychology of liberation that manifested in everyday life.

Their way of knowing was rooted in experience, embodied and African, even as it adapted to the American context. Yet, for generations, Western systems insisted that authorities must give knowledge. My people knew better: knowledge was something we discovered through endurance, reflection, and adaptability. It was earned, not simply handed down. In this regard, my personal journey is not a departure from the Dingle legacy; it's its continuation.

Like many African Americans of my generation, I inherited Western institutions, especially Christianity, not as a choice but as a cultural expectation. The church was a prominent part of Southern life. Faith was the currency of dignity, and Sunday mornings provided us with a sanctuary from a world that often felt unwelcoming.

But at some point, I noticed a rift. I sensed that the God presented to me out of fear didn't align with the God I had always known through my experiences. The doctrines spoke of separation, judgment, and seeking salvation outside of me. Yet, the tidal creeks had taught me that divinity exists within creation, not apart from it.

The water didn't ask me to believe in it. It called on me to pay attention. The wind didn't demand that I worship it; it offered

4

connection. The land didn't condemn me; it supported me. And my ancestors didn't preach; they showed me the way through their lives. This transformation, from external beliefs to internal understanding, was gradual, like the slow rise of the tide. I came to realize that faith founded on doctrine demands obedience, while faith rooted in observation fosters understanding. One binds; the other liberates. And so, my journey of self-realization began.

The most significant shift in my life happened when I reconsidered the foundations of my understanding, not merely accepting what I had been told about God but reconnecting with what I had always felt. Western views often emphasize hierarchies, separation, and linear progression. In contrast, African perspectives embrace interconnectedness, balance, and renewal. The distinction is striking: In the Western worldview, the divine resides somewhere out there. In the African worldview, the divine exists within us. Returning to an understanding rooted in African traditions didn't require me to abandon the church; it simply demanded that I reclaim my voice and narrative.

A Journey Through Tradition

For many African American families, including mine, the foundation of our early lives in America was built on faith, an inheritance that no one could strip away. It served as a steady rhythm beneath days filled with brutality, uncertainty, and survival. I think about Cato, my 4th great-grandfather, who found himself thrust into bondage. The Christianity he encountered wasn't the faith of his ancestors; it was something foreign and imposed. Yet, within the limitations of his situation, he found ways to cling to an older truth. He learned to adapt to this new religion, bending it just enough to keep the quiet voice of his inner knowing alive. He prayed as he was instructed, but he listened to the teachings of his ancestors, keeping alive a faith that served as a mask for survival, covering a deeper awareness that could never be taken from him.

Then came Sandy and Dublin, my thrice-great-grandfather and 2nd-great-grandfather, who experienced a transformation in their relationship with faith. The church evolved from a strict doctrine into a warm gathering place, offering not just spiritual guidance but also literacy instruction and structure to their often-chaotic lives. Sunday mornings were filled with songs that flowed like African melodies but echoed Christian themes, filled with rhythms and calls that resonated with their heritage.

Their faith became both a shield and a language, allowing them to embrace their dignity in a society that often undermined it. Even within the church's walls, the whispers of old ways lingered, intuition shared from grandmother to child, dreams that hinted at both trouble and blessing, and remedies drawn from the earth. While their belief in God was sincere, it coexisted with a deeper wisdom that transcended any written doctrine.

As the 20th century progressed, my grandfather Jessie, my father Isaac, and their peers navigated a world where faith shifted from mere survival to a quest for respectability and identity. The church stood as a cornerstone, a space for reclaiming honor and nurturing leadership, while also serving as a moral foundation. Nonetheless, unspoken questions lingered. Why did God only spoke through preachers? Why were some truths more profound than what Sunday school offered? Their faith remained steadfast, but a subtle shift began to emerge, realizing that their lived experiences carried just as much significance as the sermons they heard.

The significant turning point arrived after the Civil Rights Movement. As our world expanded, my family ventured into new territories, education, travel, military service, leadership, and intellectual pursuits that our ancestors could hardly imagine. It was then that faith, which had once been an anchor, started to evolve into something more personal and insightful.

Conversations that used to be kept private were now discussed openly, while seeking outside approval became less important, and interest in spirituality began to grow. Our generation began to articulate the tension between the church's teachings and the recognition of our souls. We realized that spirituality could exist beyond traditional religious boundaries, that Divinity could be experienced through awareness and intuition. Those personal encounters could illuminate truths beyond what any doctrine could express.

For the first time, African American families began to embrace faith as something more than a rigid belief system handed down through generations. It transformed into an inner witness feeling, a recognition, a deep understanding. People sought alignment rather than blind obedience. They learned to sense God within themselves instead of waiting for divine intervention from outside. This shift opened new pathways for future generations.

Today, younger people are engaging with spirituality in a markedly unique way. They honor the church, but they are not confined by it. They put faith in intuition, practice mindfulness, delve into ancestral wisdom, and see spirituality as something to be lived rather than preached. They navigate the unknown without the fear that dominated earlier generations. Their faith is not a transaction; it's an experience, chosen through resonance rather than inherited by force. They feel the echoes of their ancestors but express those sentiments in ways that resonate with their contemporary lives.

Over the years, our family's journey through faith has shifted from imposed religion to chosen community, from practiced obedience to lived wisdom, and finally from outward devotion to inward truth. This evolution didn't occur overnight or through a rejection of the past. It has been a gradual remembrance of the unseen truths that our earliest ancestors understood but could not articulate.

In those early days, my family survived through faith, but now it thrives through inner knowing. What once served as a tool for survival is now a pathway to self-realization. Cato planted the seed of this journey. Sandy and Dublin nurtured it. Jessie and Isaac questioned it. My generation awakened it. And today's youth embody it with the confidence their ancestors could only dream of. This is the spiritual arc of my family's story: a powerful evolution from inherited faith to a knowing that rises from deep within.

Cycles of change.

The air was thick with the scent of pine as the sun filtered gently through the trees, casting dappled shadows on the ground beneath Cato Dingle's feet. In the serene hush of a South Carolina grove, he felt the weight of the world lift, if only for a moment, as he whispered hopes to an expanse that seemed to listen. This grove, a sacred space for Cato and his dreams, became a symbol of resilience, grounding him amidst the challenges ahead. Cato, along with his wife, Selina, began the family's resilient journey in 1797, facing trials that tested their resolve. Though they were perceived as property by a cruel society, they dared to hold onto their homeland identity, their faith, and their dreams. Their fight was not just about survival but was a declaration of their inherent value and dignity. Cato and Selina's courage set an example for those who followed. Their strength became the family's foundation.

In 1817, Sandy and Racheal Dingle, my thrice-great-grandparents, continued that legacy, their candles flickering like the steadfast spirit within them. Despite the harshness of their work, the light from their cottage window was a beacon of hope and determination, illuminating the path for their children. They remained determined and built meaningful lives, passing this spirit to the next generation.

I was born under the same Southern sun, on Sullivan's Island, South Carolina, where my ancestors' hopes lingered. As a child, I felt both fear and faith passed down from those before me. Sitting in a pew at Mount Zion A.M.E. church, sunlight shining through stained glass, voices sang old songs. I prayed to an image unlike myself and wondered about my connection to the God I was taught to love. When I asked my mother why we prayed to someone who didn't look like us, she said, "Because our faith is bigger than any picture. Remember, you come from people who always found their own way to God." Her words sparked my desire to find faith rooted in my own heritage.

Today, my family honors this heritage through storytelling, traditional music, dances, and a family journal where everyone contributes reflections. These practices help us keep our faith vibrant and deeply connected to who we are. As I matured, I realized that true freedom means seeing my own value and honoring my roots. The Dingle story is about surviving hardships, claiming our self-worth, and developing self-leadership. Our story evolved from breaking physical chains to freeing our spirits. My path is shaped by my commitment to connection, balance, and self-awareness, values I learned from my ancestors.

I now see myself as a bridge from the past to the future. My purpose is not just to inherit my family's story but to become an ancestor who advances our legacy. My message is: We are shaped by the stories and values we choose to remember and embody, not by others' definitions. Each of us can change our self-image by looking within and embracing our past. Our legacy is defined by the awareness and understanding we create and pass on. In this journey, I am both learning and teaching. My writings are shaped by my family's enduring strength and love, and I invite you to reflect on your own story and growth.

Inner standing

Throughout human history and within my own family's journey, there has always been a fundamental choice between two ways of living. The first path is about seeking understanding within oneself, cultivating self-awareness, and a sense of peace that comes from honest observation and reflection. This inner approach leads to a lasting sense of completeness. The second path is about seeking fulfillment outside of us, chasing happiness through achievements, possessions, or the approval of others. This outward pursuit often begins subtly, as we move from knowing our true selves to defining our identity by how we appear to others. What path do you choose when the world names you? How do you reconcile the call to look inward with the pressure to conform outwardly? These questions invite you to join the conversations, echoing the theme of dual consciousness that shapes our collective journey.

My grandmother once cautioned me, saying, 'Boy, don't let the world put a label on your worth. You're more than anyone else's opinion. Listen to the quiet voice inside you, the one that knows your true name.' Her words remain a guiding light, reminding me of the dangers of letting external validation define my self-esteem. This wisdom taught me that real value comes from within, not from what others acknowledge on the outside.

As time goes on, many people believe that true happiness lies in external validation. The individual, once guided by inner wisdom, begins to measure their worth by outward successes. The constant pressure to compete drowns out intuition, and the marketplace of desires replaces the sacred space within the heart. This pattern creates what is called the fatal paradigm. The fatal paradigm is a mindset where self-worth depends entirely on external achievements or approval, promising that the next significant accomplishment or possession will finally bring peace. Yet, peace never truly arrives. For example, in my own life, I remember working tirelessly for a prestigious award, believing it would make me feel complete. But when I finally received it, the satisfaction was fleeting, and I was left searching for the next goal. The fatal paradigm thrives wherever faith in oneself is forgotten, leading us to mistake busy activity for genuine meaning and motion for true fulfillment. It places you in a perpetual external pursuit of worth, which could never be achieved. Reflecting on this, I ask you: What achievements have you pursued in the hope of finding peace, only to discover it wasn't enough? Could inner wisdom offer a path to deeper fulfillment?

This abstract idea takes on real weight in the context of family history and broader society. For generations, my family, like many others, endured systems such as slavery, segregation, and economic exploitation, designed to reinforce the fatal paradigm. These structures taught people that true power and worth were always held by someone else. By the oppressor, the church hierarchy, the law, or those who controlled wealth. Despite these external restrictions, a paradox emerged: while bodies were confined, the inner world grew resilient and strong. I recall stories of my great-grandfather, who, though denied the right to vote, would gather his children at night and speak of his dreams for their future. In these quiet moments, dignity and hope flourished, untouched by the fatal paradigm.

Our family's singing in the fields, whispering midnight prayers, and passing down quiet dignity from parent to child became a silent rebellion against the belief that meaning could only come from external approval. These practices affirmed that the deepest sense of self comes from within, not from the opinions of experts or doctrine. This inner tradition sustained our lineage for two centuries, showing the enduring power of inner knowing. For instance, my aunt Rose once told me how, during tough times, she would close her eyes and recall the hymns her mother sang, feeling strength rise inside her even when the world outside seemed harsh and unwelcoming.

Every external pursuit of self-worth carries the risk of disappointment. When meaning is placed outside oneself, it depends on circumstances that inevitably change. The soul grows restless, addicted to the chase, and fearful of stillness. In uncertain times, faith can devolve into superstition, and love becomes conditional: "I'll love you if you love me, or I love you if you're lovely". Truth, too, may be reduced to mere opinion.

Humanity loses its inner compass and mistakes the world's noise for the voice within. At the heart of this struggle is a split between two aspects of identity: the "I," representing ego, ambition, anxiety, and competitiveness, and the "I Am," signifying calmness, wholeness, and enduring existence. Let me share a personal moment of doubt that profoundly illustrated this conflict: One night, I found myself walking quietly through the dimly lit streets, weary from a day spent chasing approval and achievements. I felt overwhelmed by the pressure to conform, and the weight of inadequacy overshadowed my sense of self. As I sat down on the steps of an old, familiar building, a stillness surrounded me, and I realized that my actual value was not tied to external success but to the simple fact of being. When guided by the ego, identity centers on performance and achievement, leading to a cycle of striving driven by feelings of insufficiency.

In contrast, an awakened soul builds identity through genuine presence, recognizing worthiness as inherent and grounded in abundance rather than lack. A key factor in this dynamic is the balance between the masculine and feminine principles. The masculine principle refers to the drive to act, accomplish, and exhibit traits such as ambition, resilience, and leadership. For example, my father's determination to build a home for our family, even when resources were scarce, embodies this energy.

The feminine principle, on the other hand, represents reflection, receptivity, and nurturing qualities such as empathy, intuition, and emotional support. My mother's way of listening deeply and bringing comfort during times of loss illustrates the feminine principle at work. When these two principles are balanced, action guided by compassion, ambition tempered by empathy, life becomes both purposeful and fulfilling.

However, when the masculine principle runs unchecked, society may become overly focused on achievement, domination, and technological progress, while neglecting emotional and spiritual needs. This imbalance leads to disconnection and emptiness. For instance, a relative of mine rose quickly in his career but found himself feeling isolated and restless, realizing that success without emotional connection felt hollow. Without the feminine heart guiding the masculine will, humanity builds systems lacking compassion and advances without purpose, a world that is technologically brilliant but spiritually impoverished.

My family experiences have taught me that survival and creativity rely on this vital balance. The masculine provides strength; the feminine brings renewal. Without both, even success feels hollow. To move beyond limited perspectives, we must shift from asking, "What can I gain?" to "What can I observe?" Cultivating awareness, rather than chasing symbols of success, leads to genuine engagement. A story my grandmother, Ella, once told me comes to mind: during a season of hardship, she focused on nurturing her garden, finding simple joy, and meaning in tending the earth. That quiet act reminded her and taught me that inner wholeness gives purpose to every action. An action that I continually practice.

The most significant consequence of the fatal paradigm is not outright failure, but forgetfulness, a cloud of self-awareness that causes us to overlook our intrinsic qualities. In this paradigm, the drive to dominate and achieve often overshadows the need to reflect and nurture, resulting in a world that is outwardly developed but inwardly impoverished. The cure is not to deny the world, but to remember the self within it. My family's story is proof that meaning cannot be bought, inherited, or imposed; it must be uncovered through reflection and remembrance.

Breaking the code

There's a story of souls who refused to let external forces define their inner worth, passing down resilience and quiet strength from generation to generation. They remind me that freedom is not something bestowed; it is realized from within. Wholeness isn't found in the marketplace; it is uncovered in the heart. Transcending limiting paradigms means taking active responsibility for our lives, recognizing that our actions and perspectives shape our journey. Turning inward brings clarity to our search for meaning; greater self-awareness dispels misconceptions that cloud our sense of direction.

At such moments, we realize that purpose was never truly absent; it was simply waiting to be remembered. Social foundations and moral rules shape behavior and collective understanding. Social norms act as invisible guidelines, helping people distinguish right from wrong, success from failure, and inclusion from exclusion. When these norms are grounded in fairness and compassion, they foster unity and well-being. But when they are distorted by prejudice or injustice, they lose their protective power and can harm society rather than help it.

Social pathology is a term referring to the breakdown or sickness of a society's moral structure. It happens when the systems and rules meant to promote well-being start harming certain groups.

For example, social pathology is evident in practices like racial segregation, where people were separated in schools, restaurants, and public spaces based on race, and in discriminatory policing, where people of color are unfairly targeted and treated more harshly by law enforcement. These are not just isolated problems; they are symptoms of deeper issues in the way society is organized and governed. Social pathology shows itself most clearly when institutions create or reinforce exclusion, exploitation, or the dehumanization of certain groups, undermining the idea that all people are equally valuable.

A significant cause of social pathology in American history is the concept of white hegemony. (Okun & Tema, 1999) White hegemony means the dominance of white people and their values in shaping what is seen as "normal," "civilized," or even "divinely favored." This dominance was reinforced by various institutions, religion, law, and economics, which worked together to make whiteness the standard for intelligence, morality, and worth. At the same time, Blackness was frequently labeled as inferior or dangerous. For instance, laws once prohibited Black people from voting or owning property, and religious leaders sometimes used scripture to justify inequality. The result was a rigid hierarchy in which some lives were valued more than others, presented as natural or even ordained. Enslaved Africans and their descendants were forced to live under a system that publicly claimed to be moral, while systematically denying them fundamental rights and dignity.

Distinct historical eras mark the story of African Americans in the United States, each presenting new challenges and opportunities for resistance. After the Civil War, the Reconstruction era (1865–1877) offered a brief window of hope. During this period, formerly enslaved people gained some political and social rights, and communities began to build schools and churches. (African Americans and Education During Reconstruction: The Tolson's Chapel Schools, n.d.) However, this progress was short-lived. As Reconstruction ended, the Jim Crow era (late 1800s to mid-1900s) saw the rise of harsh segregation laws and widespread discrimination. African Americans faced violence, disenfranchisement, and economic hardship, but they also developed robust networks of support and activism.

Despite these oppressive conditions, the spirit of resilience continued to grow. During the Civil Rights Movement of the 1950s and 1960s, African Americans led a nationwide struggle to dismantle segregation and demand justice. This movement was built on the foundation of earlier generations' resistance and drew on deep wells of faith and community strength. As Dr. Martin Luther King Jr. famously declared, "Injustice anywhere is a threat to justice everywhere." (Letter from Birmingham Jail, 1963) His words reflected a long tradition of moral courage, as individuals and communities risked their lives to confront unfair laws and reshape the nation's conscience.

Throughout these eras, African American communities demonstrated remarkable resilience and creativity in the face of social pathology. For example, during the Jim Crow era, Black churches served as sanctuaries where people could organize, worship, and find hope. The songs sung in these churches— spirituals that spoke of suffering and deliverance- became anthems of freedom. The story of Harriet Tubman, who escaped slavery and led hundreds to freedom along the Underground Railroad, shows how faith and determination could overcome even the most brutal systems. Tubman once said, "I never ran my train off the track, and I never lost a passenger," a testament to her unwavering commitment to liberation. ("The passing of Harriet Tubman") (Harriet Tubman Quotes: Six Sayings to Celebrate Abolitionist On 105th Anniversary of Her Death, 2025).

Similarly, Rosa Parks's activism, which led her to refuse to give up her bus seat in Montgomery, Alabama, sparked a mass movement that changed the course of history. Parks later reflected, "I would like to be remembered as a person who wanted to be free... so other people would also be free." ("Rosa Parks: 'I would like to be remembered as a person who wanted to be ...'") (Rosa Parks quote: I would like to be remembered as a person who..., n.d.) These stories, along with countless others, highlight how moral renewal often begins with personal acts of courage and a refusal to accept unjust norms.

Although much progress has been made, the legacy of social pathology continues to affect American life. Today, issues like discriminatory policing, economic inequality, and cultural bias are reminders that harmful norms persist within institutions. Yet, the resilience that sustained previous generations continues to inspire new leaders, educators, and artists who work for justice. Programs that encourage dialogue, the rise of Black voices in literature and media, and grassroots organizing all reflect ongoing efforts to create a society rooted in equality and respect.

To further embody the legacy of resilience, families can engage by participating in local community programs that advocate civil rights and social justice. They can volunteer with organizations dedicated to social change or support initiatives focused on education and empowerment for underserved communities. Moreover, families can bolster the movement for equality by supporting Black literature, ensuring that stories of resilience and triumph are read and shared widely. This might include attending book readings by Black authors, joining book clubs that focus on African American literature, or donating to libraries to expand their collections of works by Black writers.

Additionally, families can join local initiatives that promote inclusiveness and cultural appreciation, such as arts festivals, heritage workshops, or discussion groups focused on dismantling systemic inequalities. By actively participating in these activities, families contribute to a legacy of resilience and pave the way for future generations to continue the work toward a fair and just society.

In a world overflowing with screens, slogans, and sound bites, the truth often becomes lost in a sea of distraction. Consider the phrase, "Let's check in to see how conditioned your mind really is," a mirror that challenges us not only to question what we believe but to examine why we hold those beliefs deeply. Societal conditioning, like a silent architect, subtly shapes our perceptions, emotions, and reactions over time. The essential question is not whether we are conditioned, but how deeply that conditioning has seeped into our understanding.

Reflecting on a moment from my own life, I recall the first time I encountered an advertisement that made me question my cultural beauty. I was an impressionable teenager, mesmerized by a commercial showcasing flawless models who were nothing like the people in my life whom I admired for their strength and resilience. This single image sowed seeds of doubt and made me question my own worth. It was a subtle yet powerful nudge, leading me to believe that beauty was a narrow concept defined by someone else's standards rather than the rich, diverse reality of my heritage. This moment was a personal turning point, revealing how marketing can steer our self-perception and influence our ideals without us even realizing it. Such experiences lay bare the power of conditioning and illuminate their pervasive reach.

A striking warning comes from scripture: "If the light in you be darkness, how great is that darkness" (Matthew 6:23, NKJV). This message reminds us that when our inner guidance, our moral and spiritual compass, is warped, the resulting darkness within us can be profound. In everyday life, distorted conditioning can cloud our judgment and erode our sense of right and wrong.

Every morning, before many Americans finish their first cup of coffee, marketing messages flood their consciousness. Take the iconic "Got Milk?" campaign, which transformed milk from a basic grocery item into a symbol of health and coolness through celebrity endorsements and catchy slogans. Or consider Apple's "Think Different" ads, which didn't just sell computers; they sold you an identity of innovation and nonconformity. These campaigns demonstrate how corporations invest billions to cultivate our cravings, influence our clothing choices, and shape the standards by which we measure success. Algorithms now amplify this effect, tracking our digital footprints to tailor advertisements that seamlessly blend with our interests, sometimes making us question whether our desires are genuinely our own. The marketplace, in this sense, becomes a modern puppeteer, quietly steering our tastes and behaviors with invisible strings.

Just as marketing manipulates our desires, politics employs similar techniques to harness our loyalties and shape public opinion. Political campaigns often use emotionally charged slogans, think "Make America Great Again" or "Yes We Can," to foster a sense of belonging or urgency. Media outlets frame issues in ways that provoke instant reactions: instead of encouraging thoughtful analysis, coverage often stirs outrage or fear. The language of politics, filled with "us versus them" rhetoric, primes citizens to cheer for parties rather than question policies. This interplay between marketing and politics reveals a continuum: both systems rely on conditioning to prompt automatic responses, making it harder for individuals to pause, reflect, and engage critically.

The thread of conditioning winds further into the realm of emotion, which is the oldest and most potent form of programming. Emotional appeals are central to both advertising ("Because You're Worth It" L'Oréal) and political speeches, designed to inspire loyalty or incite anger. When institutionalized, religion can harness emotions as well, sometimes crossing the line from spiritual guidance into manipulation. For example, the use of guilt or fear in sermons, or the promise of salvation for obedience, can lead congregants to conform without questioning. Yet, faith at its best can liberate the spirit; think of the story of Moses leading the Israelites out of Egypt, a narrative of awakening and freedom from oppressive conditioning. The boundary between liberation and manipulation is delicate and easily crossed.

These domains of marketing, politics, emotion, and religion are interwoven in the tapestry of our daily lives, each reinforcing the other's influence. From the moment we wake up to the headlines on our phones, to the commercials on our screens, to the political debates we overhear, each sphere nudges us toward a particular way of seeing the world. Together, they form a network of conditioning that can be difficult to escape. The question remains: how deeply has your conditioning shaped you? In an era defined by rapid change and automation, many people experience profound shifts, becoming more informed yet less self-aware, more connected but less conscious of themselves. The path to autonomy begins not with rebellion, but with self-observation: noticing what triggers us, questioning our reactions, and seeking the roots of our beliefs.

Popular culture continually explores this dilemma. The metaphor from the film "The Matrix"—the choice between a red pill and a blue pill—captures the tension between accepting a comfortable illusion and embracing a painful truth. Similarly, Plato's Allegory of the Cave describes individuals who mistake shadows for reality until one dare to understand something clearly at last. (Red pill and blue pill, n.d.) Historical examples abound: the Civil Rights Movement challenged the conditioned norms of segregation, demanding Americans awaken to justice and equality. Each of these stories illustrates the possibility and the challenge of breaking free from conditioned thinking.

Every individual faces the choice: to remain comfortably conditioned or to awaken to deeper consciousness. In a society saturated with persuasive influences, the journey toward truth demands vigilance, self-reflection, and the courage to question even our most beliefs. Only by recognizing and confronting the forces that shape us can we hope to reclaim our autonomy, transforming passive acceptance into conscious awareness.

Finding your place

Consider the rhythmic heartbeat of drumming at dawn and the sacred ritual of liberation at dusk. These practices create living connections with ancestors and spirits, grounding individuals into a profound understanding of the universe. They invite us to explore unity and purpose through deeply rooted traditions that affirm our place in the cosmos. This lived experience answers the existential questions of origin, structure, and destiny, uniquely reflecting an interconnected worldview.

Cosmology, in a broader sense, examines the universe's origins, structure, development, and ultimate destiny. It seeks to answer foundational questions: Where did everything begin? How is the universe organized? What is humanity's place in this vast expanse?

In traditional African thought, cosmology is not just an abstract concept, but a living reality interwoven into daily life. It includes both the unseen world, ancestors, spirits, and the divine, and the visible world of nature, community, and the individual. (Mojo bag, n.d.) This worldview emphasizes the interconnectedness of all things, establishing a spiritual and moral order that guides behavior and shape's identity. For example, communal rituals such as the Yoruba Egungun festival celebrate ancestors and reinforce bonds within the community, illustrating how cosmology operates through shared practices. These ceremonies remind participants that their well-being is tied to both the living and the departed, nurturing a sense of unity and continuity.

For people of African descent, cosmology has special importance due to histories of displacement and cultural disruption. It becomes a mirror for self-identity, reflecting both loss and the potential for renewal. The introduction of Western influences often redefined identity, sometimes resulting in "double consciousness." Double consciousness, as described by W.E.B. Du Bois, refers to the internal conflict individuals experience as they navigate multiple cultural identities, torn between their ancestral heritage and the expectations of a dominant culture. (The Souls of Black Folk, 1903) This tension can lead to feelings of alienation. Yet, within the African cosmological framework, existence remains sacred and intimately linked to ancestors, with the ongoing goal of restoring balance among self, community, nature, and the divine.

Cosmology also provides a structure for self-understanding and personal growth. African cosmology emphasizes harmony and interdependence, encouraging individuals to see themselves as part of a living continuum. I vividly remember our family's communal naming ceremony for my nephew, where everyone gathered to affirm his identity and role within the family. My elder brother led the prayer, weaving in stories from our ancestors, while other family members prepared the traditional dish that symbolized unity. This event embodied the principle of Ubuntu, where 'I am because we are,' underscoring the deep connection between individual identity and community support. In contrast, Western cosmology often takes a more mechanistic and individualistic approach. Western societies may prioritize personal achievement, as seen in graduation ceremonies or entrepreneurial success stories, which highlight individual milestones rather than communal bonds. This focus on individualism can sometimes lead to a fragmented sense of self if not balanced by deeper social or spiritual connections.

Throughout history, African cosmology has functioned as a powerful tool for resilience and renewal. During the era of the transatlantic slave trade, enslaved Africans carried their cosmological beliefs to the Americas, transforming them into new practices such as the Ring Shout in the United States or Candomblé in Brazil. (Hoodoo (spirituality), n.d.) These traditions blended ancestral wisdom with new realities, preserving a sense of spiritual sovereignty, the right and ability to define one's spiritual life independently, despite external pressures. For example, the continued honoring of ancestors in African American church services, or the use of spirituals as coded messages of freedom, reflect how cosmology helped communities endure hardship and reclaim their sense of belonging.

When individuals reconnect with their roots through language, art, ritual, or history, they engage in what can be called a "cosmological act." A cosmological act is any action that restores alignment between one's inner sense of self and the broader cosmic order. For instance, when African diaspora communities revive traditional festivals, learn ancestral languages, or create art inspired by their heritage, they are not just celebrating culture; they are actively reconstructing their universe and reaffirming their place within it. Ultimately, truly knowing oneself means understanding one's place within creation. For those whose histories have been interrupted, reclaiming their space in the universe is both a liberating and healing process. By embracing cosmological principles, individuals and communities can restore balance, recover meaning, and sustain a sense of belonging within the cosmos.

Section Two:

In the age of awareness

Transitioning from Section One, which roots us in self-discovery and cultural heritage, we move into Section Two: In the Age of Awareness. Here, we examine how awakening and heightened consciousness shape identity, community, and the pursuit of truth. Leaving foundational questions behind, we explore what happens when individuals and communities view themselves and the world anew.

Crisis of Consciousness

In an Afrocentric worldview, origins are not mere abstractions; they are the heartbeat of existence, the pulse that connects heaven and earth, spirit and matter, ancestors, and descendants. This seamless continuum underscores the sacredness and order of the universe, where every element holds meaning and purpose. At the center of this cosmic order stands Ma'at, the ancient Egyptian principle embodying truth, justice, balance, and cosmic order. (Maat, n.d.) In ancient Egypt, Ma'at was revered as the force that maintained harmony in both society and the universe; living in accordance with Ma'at meant upholding truth and fairness in every thought, word, and deed. Humanity, from this perspective, is not separated from the cosmos but is its living expression. To live authentically is to align with these divine principles. Yet, when one's cosmological foundation falls out of sync with lived experience, a profound existential disturbance arises, recognized today as a crisis of consciousness.

Imagine the following scene:

Ancestral voice: Remember Ma'at, for it is the path of truth and balance.

Your voice: But how do I find balance when my world seems so disjointed?

Ancestral voice: Seek within the traditions and wisdom passed down through the ages.

Your voice: With so much change and chaos, how do I hold on to what is true?

Ancestral voice: Ground yourself in the principles of Ma'at; they will guide you even in turmoil.

Before colonialism swept across Africa, cosmologies such as those of the Kemet (ancient Egypt), Yoruba, Akan, and Zulu peoples were grounded in deep relationships and interconnectedness. Ma'at guided the north, while Ubuntu shaped the south. Ubuntu is a Southern African philosophy emphasizing communal interdependence and humanity toward others, captured in the phrase, "I am because we are." (Ubuntu philosophy, n.d.) In the West, the Yoruba followed Ifa, a divination system and spiritual philosophy that interprets the will of the cosmos through sacred verses, guiding moral choices and daily life. (Ifa divination system, 2008) These diverse yet interwoven belief systems upheld a fundamental truth: "I am because we are, and we are because the universe is." Such principles instilled a profound sense of belonging, with ancestors seen as living presences guiding the community's moral direction, the earth revered as a nurturing mother, and community considered the natural condition of existence.

The arrival of colonial powers and the transatlantic slave trade violently disrupted this cosmic harmony. Colonial authorities replaced Indigenous spiritual practices with Christianity, often outlawing ancestral rituals and demonizing traditional beliefs.

For example, colonial governments imposed new social structures, appointing chiefs loyal to European rule and dismantling communal leadership. Missionaries taught only selective parts of the Bible, emphasizing obedience and submission, while suppressing local languages and cosmologies. The sacred principle of oneness was fractured as foreign gods and hierarchies redefined human worth. These actions not only enslaved African bodies but also sought to enslave African minds and spirits, erasing the cosmological foundation that had anchored generations.

A crisis of consciousness emerges when cosmological views collide with lived realities. This struggle goes beyond psychology; it cuts to the core of personal identity. W. E. B. Du Bois described this experience as double consciousness: the internal conflict of being shaped by ancestral traditions while navigating a society rooted in racial hierarchy. (W. E. B. DuBois, 1903) The breakdown occurs when self-understanding, once grounded in spiritual and communal traditions, is challenged by systems that undermine those beliefs. Frantz Fanon called this state "the colonized mind," referring to the alienation and confusion experienced when one's original self is suppressed by imposed narratives and values. (Frantz Fanon – Roots and Narcissism, n.d.) Even material success cannot resolve this deep spiritual dislocation; the oppressed may worship a god foreign to their ancestors, follow a morality that diminishes their being, and seek validation from systems that do not honor their truth. This is the deepest wound

36

of colonialism: the forced adoption of a narrative that negates the essence of the oppressed.

On a personal level, losing touch with ancestral cosmology leads to inner fragmentation, a rift between intuitive, inherited wisdom and beliefs acquired under pressure. The search for identity becomes a quest for cosmic belonging, a longing to recover what has been lost but not destroyed. Collectively, this fragmentation weakens the community's moral and spiritual fabric. As cultural memory fades, foreign ideals are imitated in place of ancestral wisdom. The sacred bonds among people, ancestors, and the land, so central to African cosmology, are commodified or neglected, leaving communities vulnerable to further disruption.

This crisis is not limited to questions of race or politics; it is profound homelessness, a spiritual exile that calls for healing through reestablishing one's place in creation. Afrocentric thought teaches that genuine liberation comes from restoring cosmological foundations. This means reclaiming Ma'at (truth and balance), restoring moral and spiritual order, embracing Ubuntu (humanity through relationship and reciprocity), and honoring ancestors as vital members of the spiritual family. By centering African thought, aesthetics, and spirituality in education, art, governance, and daily life, belief becomes a living reality, enabling the sacred once again to guide social, political, and economic life. When these principles are restored, cosmological reality is provided to empower individuals to become architects of their own worlds, rather than mere reflections in another's universe.

When original foundations are at odds with everyday practice, identity fractures and crises of consciousness inevitably follow. The human spirit cannot thrive in contradiction. Yet within this crisis lies the possibility of awakening, a call to restore balance and wholeness. For people of African descent, this awakening comes through recognizing themselves not as orphans of history, but as descendants of a divine lineage that understood the harmony between heaven and earth. Living by Ma'at, acting through Ubuntu, and honoring ancestors is the path to reconciling belief with being, faith with reality, and soul with society. This journey marks the end of alienation and signals a return to the fullness of the African cosmos, whole, centered, and free.

In Plain View

This is my reflection on how faith, culture, and self-knowledge have helped generations of African descendants endure and thrive from slavery to today. My family's story, like that of many African Americans, is woven from a spiritual journey that stretches across continents and centuries, shaped by both ancestral memory and Western religious tradition.

To understand this journey, it's essential to clarify some key ideas. Afrocentricity is a way of thinking and seeing the world that puts African people, their history, culture, and experiences at the center of their own stories. Coined by scholars like Dr. Molefi Kete Asante, it means interpreting life through African eyes rather than through the lens of outsiders. (Asante & Kete, 1980) For example, instead of only learning about Africa from European textbooks, Afrocentricity encourages us to value African oral histories, art, and spiritual practices as equally important sources of knowledge.

Decolonization is the process of undoing the influence and control of colonial powers, especially in culture, education, and religion. (Muasya & Njeri, 2020). In the context of religion, decolonization means challenging and transforming beliefs, rituals, and church structures that were shaped by colonial rule, such as rejecting teachings that demand blind submission or erase African cultural expressions. It asks tough questions: Whose version of

Christianity are we practicing? Whose interests does it serve? Decolonizing faith is about reclaiming spiritual practices that honor both ancestor and community, not just the authority of former colonizers.

.

Re-Africanization goes a step further. It means actively bringing African values, symbols, and rituals back into religious and cultural life. In a church setting, for example, re-Africanization might include African drumming, dance, or languages in worship services, making space for expressions of faith that reflect African heritage rather than only European traditions.

The relationship between Afrocentric thought and Christianity is complex. For many African Americans, it's not just an academic debate; it's a profoundly personal question about spiritual and cultural identity. Can we embrace our Africanness while practicing a religion that came with colonialism and slavery? Is it possible for Christianity to change, through decolonization and re-Africanization, so that it uplifts, rather than suppresses, African identity? And can Afrocentricity, in turn, find room for the spiritual principles that have helped our ancestors survive hardship and oppression?

History shows that Christianity arrived in Africa and the Americas as both a tool of liberation and a weapon of oppression. European missionaries, supported by colonial authorities, often equated Christianity with "civilization" and condemned African spiritual practices as superstitious or evil. (Colonial Legacies: Slavery, Christianity, and the Transformation of Indigenous Liberian Religious-Cultural Identities, 2023) They replaced the African worldview, one that was holistic, communal, and cyclical, with a more rigid, divided theology.

In America, enslaved Africans were taught a version of Christianity that emphasized obedience, as in the "Master's Bible," which included lines like, "Servants, obey your masters." The Bible was used to justify slavery. Then Africans made Christianity their path to freedom. But even in these circumstances, enslaved people found messages of hope and deliverance, stories of Moses and Jesus that they made their own.

This was the beginning of the re-Africanization of Christianity. Despite its arrival in chains, African people reshaped the faith with their own rhythms, memories, and meanings. Spirituals, call-and-response worship, and heartfelt testimony transformed Christianity from a religion of the oppressor into a theology of the oppressed. A living example can be found in the African Methodist Episcopal (A.M.E.) Church, founded by Richard Allen in 1816. Here, Black faith flourished under Black leadership, blending prayers and sermons with African musical traditions and communal support. In some A.M.E. churches today, you might witness a "libation ceremony," in which water is poured, and prayers are offered to honor the ancestors, an African ritual woven into Christian worship. This is re-Africanization in action: affirming that spiritual roots run deeper than colonial history.

A vivid example comes from the story of a congregation in Chicago's South Side. During Sunday services, elders lead a procession carrying kente cloths and drums, and the pastor opens with a prayer that invokes both the Holy Spirit and the ancestors who "walked before us and made a way." Children learn not only Bible verses but also proverbs from West Africa, and at Easter, the church hosts a "Festival of Resurrection" with African dance and storytelling. For this community, blending African traditions with Christian worship is not just symbolic; it is an act of healing and wholeness, a way to decolonize faith and reclaim dignity.

In my own family, we had a tradition of gathering for an oyster roast or a fish fry to raise money for community support. There, you would have groups of people from the surrounding communities. My grandmother blesses the meal in both English and a few words of Gullah Geechee, the language created by my ancestors after arriving here on American shores. It wasn't strange to hear people of the Gullah, Geechee traditions, bantering back and forth with the so-called proper English speakers. It was as if they were fluent in two different languages, giving and taking in both dialects.

Throughout that time, you would hear stories about people who have passed on, remembering their wisdom and sacrifices. This ritual, part prayer, part storytelling, part celebration, embodies the heart of both Afrocentric and Christian values: honoring our elders, giving thanks, and building community across generations. These moments connect our family to broader cultural movements that seek to restore the sacred link between the past and the present, between earth and spirit.

Afrocentricity and Christianity can complement one another when approached with honesty and cultural respect. Afrocentricity insists that African people see and define themselves in their own terms, including their relationship with the divine. Decolonization challenges us to question which religious practices truly serve our spiritual needs, rather than repeating what was imposed. Re-Africanization gives us the tools and the courage to make faith our own, through music, ritual, and memory. In the end, the most powerful theology is one that honors both the ancestors and the Creator, allowing us to move freely between the language of heaven and the drumbeat of the earth.

Africa is not peripheral to the Bible; it is central. Ethiopia, Egypt, and Nubia appear throughout scripture, and early Christianity had strong roots in North and East Africa. (Dotawo, n.d.) Reading the Bible with an Afrocentric lens restores Africa's rightful place in sacred history, freeing it from Eurocentric distortion. Yet, harmony requires transformation. Christianity that clings to Eurocentric dominance cannot coexist with Afrocentric liberation. When faith demands that Africans reject their heritage, their music, or their names, it becomes an agent of oppression. Afrocentricity calls for the end of this spiritual dependency, for a Christianity that is African in voice, rhythm, and heart.

This also means that African Christians must challenge doctrines that devalue the body, the earth, or women, all which conflict with African holistic spirituality. The work of thinkers like Mercy Amba Oduwole and Desmond Tutu points to this integration: a Christianity of justice, community, and joy. Afrocentricity and Christianity need not be enemies. When stripped of its colonial baggage, Christianity can serve as a moral and spiritual framework that uplifts African identity rather than erases it. Afrocentricity, in turn, gives faith cultural depth, rooting worship in heritage, rhythm, and ancestral wisdom.

Together, they can form a theology that sings in both the language of heaven and the drumbeat of the earth. A faith that honors the ancestors while building a future of dignity and liberation. In the final measure, the proper harmony between Afrocentric thought and Christian belief lies not in opposition but in balance: the African soul walking freely, guided by both the wisdom of the ancestors and the light of divine love.

A little small thing amounts to something Big

The story of African Americans is more than a chronicle of survival and struggle; it is also the account of a profound spiritual transformation that guided this survival. (Movements, Motions, Moments: Photographs of Religion and Spirituality from the National Museum of African American History and Culture, 2023) From the earliest enslaved Africans brought to the Americas to present-day Black communities, religion and faith have continually served as both refuge and forms of resistance. There is, however, a crucial distinction to be made between religion, a structured, institutional system of belief often shaped by external forces, and faith, a profound personal conviction rooted in self-knowledge, resilience, and hope.

Over time, African Americans shifted from a dependency on religion as an imposed structure to embracing faith as a liberating force. This transition empowered them to transcend white hegemony and assert their own humanity. For enslaved Africans, religion was not simply a system of worship; it was a lifeline in a world designed to dehumanize. Many arrived with rich spiritual traditions from West and Central Africa, where the divine was intimately woven into daily life and connected to ancestors, nature, and community. (Sacred Trees & Spirit Forests: Nature in African Spiritual Cosmology, 2023) These traditions were violently disrupted by enslavement, and Christianity, especially in its slaveholder's form, was introduced as a tool of control.

Yet, enslaved Africans transformed this very tool into a weapon of resistance. Beneath the surface of plantation Christianity, they crafted a subversive theology that spoke to freedom, deliverance, and the inherent dignity of all people. Through songs, coded sermons, and secret prayer meetings known as "hush harbors," they reinterpreted biblical stories, such as those of Moses and the Exodus, as metaphors for their own deliverance. (Songs of the Underground Railroad, n.d.) Religion became the language through which enslaved people could imagine freedom, affirm their identity, and preserve their humanity under brutal conditions.

After emancipation, the newly freed population established the Black church, one of the most influential institutions in African American life. (Juneteenth and the Black Church, n.d.) Freed from white oversight, the church became the first autonomous center for Black organization, education, and politics. It was a place where people learned to read, debated moral issues, and developed leadership that would later drive the Civil Rights Movement.

This period marked the height of religious dependence, as pastors led communities, churches acted as schools, and Sunday worship became a declaration of human worth. The Black church represented what slavery had denied: a self-governed space of dignity and voice. For families in South Carolina, the church replaced the plantation as the new center of identity and social structure, guiding formerly enslaved people and women toward collective progress. (The Historic Legacy of Black Charleston Church Where Shooting Occurred, n.d.)

As Reconstruction gave way to segregation and racial violence, religion again became a shield against despair. The hymns, rituals, and traditions of the church reminded Black people that their suffering had meaning, and their survival had purpose. Religion offered emotional and communal stability in an unstable, hostile society, sustaining the collective psyche of African Americans. It provided a moral language to confront injustice and reinforced a sense of belonging to a higher order, even when earthly systems denied them justice.

During this era, a subtle shift occurred: an awareness that formal religion, often modeled after white denominations, could not fully address the realities of Black existence. Spirituals evolved into gospel songs infused with social commentary, and sermons began calling for self-determination and racial pride. This marked the early shift toward faith rather than religion, a transition from ritual observance to inner conviction and direct empowerment.

By the mid-20th century, African American spirituality had matured further. Leaders like Dr. Martin Luther King Jr.

exemplified the synthesis of religion and faith, combining institutional theology with personal moral vision. (King & Jr., 1963) Churches served as command centers of social revolution, but it was faith, an inner assurance of righteousness and destiny, which propelled ordinary people to confront injustice with courage. The Civil Rights Movement transformed Black spiritual tradition into a national moral force, asserting that justice was not only political but sacred, rooted in the unshakable faith that right would prevail over wrong. (Gamboa & Isaias, 2012) While the church remained central, the movement revealed something greater: the power of belief, courage, and unity that extended beyond doctrine or denomination.

In the decades following the Civil Rights Movement, African Americans increasingly relied on personal faith as a mode of liberation, rather than on formal religious institutions. While churches remain influential, younger generations often pursue spiritual independence, viewing God, ancestors, and the self as interconnected sources of empowerment. This modern faith is expressed through art, activism, music, and personal wellness, not solely through traditional worship. It reflects the understanding that liberation begins in the mind and heart before manifesting in society. The same spiritual energy that once fueled hush harbors now inspires self-awareness, education, and creative expression among descendants of survivors.

Today, African American faith is less dependent on external approval or religious conformity, representing an inward conviction that neither social systems nor historical wounds determine one's worth, purpose, or destiny. (Harrell & P., 2022) This faith empowers African Americans to rise above white hegemony, not through rejection or hatred, but through self-realization, excellence, and collective uplift. The journey from the religion of enslavement to the faith of self-determination is a profound transformation in African American history. Religion provided structure, hope, and survival; faith now offers freedom, creativity, and power. The enslaved believed in deliverance beyond this world, while their descendants learned to create deliverance within it. For African Americans, the evolution from religion to faith is not a rejection of God, but the reclaiming of divinity within. It is the unbroken continuation of a spiritual heritage rooted in African soil, surviving the Middle Passage, and flourishing under oppression. Today, faith stands not as dependency but as declaration: African Americans are the authors of their destiny, keepers of their spirit, and living proof that no system of power can extinguish the light within.

Section Three

What we think we know

As we conclude Section Two, focused on growing awareness and evolving consciousness, we turn to Section Three: What We Think We Know. Here, the essays move from awakening to examining the beliefs, assumptions, and knowledge systems that shape our lives. This section invites us to question accepted truths and reflect on how our perspectives are molded by personal experience and collective memory.

Is it magic?

Throughout history, humanity has sought to understand how unseen possibilities become reality. For those guided by religion, this process centers on faith, the trust that what is hoped for may happen. Scientists approach the same mystery through observation, which involves measuring and verifying existence. While faith and observation may appear distinct, both describe how consciousness interacts with reality.

Faith originates in the heart and goes beyond mere belief, acting as a unique way of perceiving possibilities. It channels energy and intention toward desired outcomes, providing emotional steadiness and fostering courage. Although faith does not guarantee specific results, it prepares individuals to receive them, shaping their readiness for what may unfold. Observation, like faith, actively shapes reality. In quantum physics, particles exist as possibilities until they are observed, at which point they become defined. This concept parallels daily life, where focused attention, whether on fear or peace, causes those qualities to grow. Observation transforms potential into experience, demonstrating where faith and awareness intersect.

Faith and observation work in tandem to approach the same mystery. Faith involves trust and emotion, while observation relies on focus and awareness. Both require conscious attention and suggest that consciousness itself influences the course of reality. Science discusses these concepts in terms of energy and probability, whereas religion speaks of spirit and promise. The beliefs we hold and the observations we make shape our lives.

Both quantum science and scripture propose that thought shapes reality. In scientific terms, faith can be understood as an "emotional inheritance," where belief, intention, and action produce observable effects. Regardless of the chosen approach, the process involves focusing, feeling, acting, and releasing with trust, a synthesis of devotion and precision. A living synthesis reveals that consciousness, whether expressed through prayer or scientific observation, can influence outcomes. Faith provides direction; observation provides form, encouraging mindful participation in shaping the world.

Generations have shown that shaping possibilities through consciousness is a consistent and enduring practice. The next step is to combine faith and observation as a mindful, conscious daily routine, integrating both principles to navigate and influence the unfolding of reality.

Leela, a quantum entanglement

Creation, at its essence, emerges not from force but from a harmonious interplay between what is visible and what is hidden, between our beliefs and our perceptions. Every meaningful act of creation, whether as vast as the universe or as subtle as a fleeting thought, originates in a place of quiet faith. It is from this silent space that ideas first take shape, and through the attentive act of observation, they are brought forth into reality. Faith and observation, rather than being opposing forces, are partners in the process of manifestation.

Faith represents the spark of divine masculinity, the initial seed of intention sown into the realm of the unseen. It is an act of declaration, affirming the existence of something before any tangible evidence appears. Faith does not seek validation; instead, it generates its own proof. With unwavering certainty, faith proclaims, "Let there be," embodying conviction rather than mere hope.

Observation serves as the mirror of divine femininity, providing a sacred space where faith is carefully nurtured into form. It is the receptive womb of consciousness, an act both gentle and powerful, allowing one to see with the heart until the intangible becomes real. Observation is marked by patience; it does not hurry but instead welcomes what is to come. It softly affirms,

"And there was," transforming potential into lived experience through quiet attentiveness.

Within everyone resides in this dynamic duality: the masculine force that initiates and the feminine grace that fosters growth. The masculine principle provides direction and projects intention outward, while the feminine principle offers depth and reflects inward. When these elements are held in balance, the process of creation is complete, ideas are conceived and nurtured, dreams take root, and what was once invisible becomes seen.

Actual creation depends on the harmonious interplay between the masculine and feminine principles. When this balance is disrupted, the process of manifestation becomes distorted. If the masculine force prevails, faith transforms into unchecked ambition, an idea compelled into existence without the tempering presence of compassion or natural rhythm. Conversely, when the feminine aspect overshadows, observation turns into passivity and endless anticipation, lacking the structure and initiative required to bring ideas into form. Authentic creation, therefore, requires both the courage to declare and the gentleness to receive, blending mental clarity with heartfelt openness.

Every thought that is held with faith and observed with love becomes a living seed, ready to grow. As with a gardener tending to their plants, it is essential to shield these seeds from the weeds of doubt and the storms of distraction. The state of one's inner being, the soil of the soul, responds to what is planted with intention. When faith is steady and observation is mindful, manifestation arises not as a miraculous event but as a natural result of alignment between spirit and matter.

A faithful observer avoids falling into the extremes of either unchecked imagination or rigid skepticism. Instead, they maintain a balance between belief and awareness, understanding that creation unfolds gradually through the union of faith and observation. These two forces are not adversaries but partners in the creative process. Living in this way means recognizing creativity as an inner journey, where what is nurtured within eventually takes shape in the outer world. When faith and observation are aligned, the invisible becomes visible, and life responds to this harmony.

The seed, the soil, and the sun

For over two centuries, my family has journeyed along a sacred path defined by the interplay of faith and manifestation. Their story is not simply one of endurance, but a living demonstration of the power to create a path where none existed before. Each generation embodied the unfolding of divine consciousness through acts of courage, holding steadfast to unseen promises and patiently observing them as they took shape. Faith became the first inheritance passed down through the generations; observation grew into the sacred practice that nurtured this faith. Together, these principles formed the unbreakable foundation of our family's lineage.

The First Observers (1797 - Early 1800s), Cato and Selina, were pioneers in envisioning possibilities in a world that refused to acknowledge their humanity. While bound by the constraints of their time, they found freedom through vision, becoming living embodiments of the harmonious balance between the divine masculine and feminine.

Cato's faith was a powerful belief in a future he could not see, a willingness to plant seeds in soil he might never harvest. Selina's observation represented the nurturing force that kept hope alive through adversity, holding the family's dreams in her heart with the gentle care of a mother. Together, they served as the first faithful observers, transforming captivity into a sacred covenant. Though they lacked the means to read the stars or own the land they tilled, their sacred intentions aligned them with a higher purpose. In their union, the family's legacy began, deeply rooted in endurance and guided by an unseen light.

The cultivators of vision (1819 – 1870s), Sandy and his wife, Racheal, carried the family's flame through the difficult era of Reconstruction. For them, faith was not merely a doctrine but a daily practice, rising before sunrise to instruct their children, labor, and rebuild what had been lost. Sandy embodied the masculine principle, offering direction and believing in self-sufficiency, learning, and the dignity found in challenging work. Racheal brought the feminine principle, imparting lessons in love, patience, and quiet perseverance. Together, they were faithful observers, nurturing the promise of freedom amid hardship and transforming the invisible into reality. Their vision was centered not on material wealth, but on wisdom, community, and continuity for future generations.

As the century turned into the early 1900s, Dublin and Martha turned their ancestors' dreams into reality. Under their leadership, the family evolved from field hands to skilled craftsmen, educators, and community leaders. Dublin's faith was assertive and protective. He possessed the drive to establish lasting foundations. Martha's observation was intuitive and compassionate, possessing the wisdom to discern when to wait and when to act. Together, they built enduring structures — homes, values, and reputations — that would be carried forward for generations. Sixty years later, their efforts bore fruit as what was once invisible began to manifest in the physical world.

Jessie and Sara Jane (1890 – 1960s) entered a turbulent America, navigating the space between oppression and opportunity. They observed their surroundings with clarity, refusing to let bitterness erode their faith. Their children were raised to stand tall, speak truthfully, and maintain dignity regardless of the difficulties they faced. Their faith provided the courage to dream even in the face of segregation, while their observation bestowed the wisdom to discern when to resist and when to rise above. In their hands, the family's resilient spirit became both protective and a strength, a faith that envisioned freedom long before it was realized.

Isaac and Dolly (1920s -2011) emerged from the enduring prayers of their ancestors as bridge builders, connecting different eras. Isaac's disciplined faith was demonstrated through leadership, service, and devotion to family. Dolly's nurturing observation was expressed in her compassion, steady faith, and the sacred cadence she established within the home. Together, they exemplified the balance of divine polarity: faith that could move mountains, and observation that tended to the garden once those mountains had shifted. Their example transformed the family home into a sanctuary of wisdom and a strong work ethic. Their faith was steady rather than loud, and their observation assertive rather than passive. Under their leadership, the family learned that true creation requires both belief in the unseen and action as if it were already visible.

The manifesters of vision, Blanche and I, stand at the intersection of tradition and transformation. In us, the family's enduring faith met new opportunities. Our drive propelled our family toward education, service, and community advancement. Blanche's grace expanded our legacy through care, creativity, and cultural pride. We do not merely hold the family's faith; we activate it, ensuring that every child and grandchild recognizes their place in an unbroken chain of divine creations. Our home became both an altar and a classroom where love, laughter, and faith were interwoven into daily life. As faithful observers of the present, we teach that true miracles are not just survival but continued thriving.

The future in Lee, Camille, and Matthew, along with London, Autumn, and Levi, represents the living outcomes of generations of dedicated observation. Their lives demonstrate that what was once considered a mere belief has now become a reality. They are bridges joining ancestral memories with future potential, the tangible embodiment of prayers once spoken in hope. Each carry within itself the masculine courage to declare "Let there be" and the feminine wisdom to wait, nurture, and love what is coming into being. Through them, the tradition of faith and observation continues, alive and unfolding as a conscious practice rather than mere history.

The family's journey highlights the significance of purposeful observation and steadfast faith. Their experience illustrates that true faith is visionary and that observation is an active, dynamic engagement with life. These qualities, combined, have enabled them to meet and overcome formidable challenges. Across war, enslavement, reconstruction, and renewal, each generation has demonstrated that genuine creation arises from conscious awareness, not privilege. Their ongoing dedication to faith and love has transformed adversity into resilience, sustaining the family through the ages.

Today, the family is honored not only for their heritage as survivors but for their commitment to actively shaping the future. Their story demonstrates that the human spirit, guided by faith and mindful observation, holds the power to influence its own destiny. To be a member of this family is to uphold a tradition of attentive observation, belief in possibility, and the nurturing of potential until it is fully realized.

Decolonize your mind

At its core, Afrocentricity is a perspective that encourages viewing the world through African eyes. Rather than interpreting African history, values, and culture through European or Western frameworks, Afrocentricity places these elements at the center of analysis. Developed by scholars such as Molefi Kete Asante, this approach emphasizes the importance of African people defining their own reality, reclaiming their narratives, and cultivating self-awareness deeply rooted in their ancestral worldview. (Asante & Kete, 1980) The central tenet is to center the African experience—not as a mere offshoot of Western history, but as a distinct civilization with its own philosophy, scientific achievements, and aesthetic traditions.

In contrast, Pan-Africanism is a political and cultural movement dedicated to uniting people of African descent worldwide. Emerging in the 19th and early 20th centuries through influential figures such as W.E.B. Du Bois, Marcus Garvey, Kwame Nkrumah, and George Padmore, Pan-Africanism advocates solidarity among Africans and the diaspora to confront colonialism, racism, and economic exploitation. (Pan-Africanism, n.d.) It calls for collective action among all African peoples—both on the continent and in the diaspora—to work together for liberation and progress.

While Afrocentricity is primarily philosophical and cultural, Pan-Africanism takes a political and organizational form. Yet, both share a common goal: the restoration of African dignity and agency. Afrocentricity begins at the level of individual consciousness, encouraging African-descended individuals to re-examine their thoughts, values, and self-perceptions in the context of history. For the Afrocentric thinker, the suffering experienced by Black people originates from dislocation—being separated from land, language, and identity, leading to a spiritual and cultural unmooring. The solution, according to Afrocentricity, is a profound return to African-centered thought, art, and behavior.

Pan-Africanism, on the other hand, operates from a collective consciousness. It is less concerned with individual re-centering and more focused on uniting the dispersed African family. Its emphasis is on structural change, regaining political power, economic control, and sovereignty for the continent. (Pan-Africanism - Wikipedia, n.d.) Pan-Africanism envisions global solidarity, connecting communities from Lagos to London, Harlem to Accra, Bahia to Dakar, and beyond. In this way, Afrocentricity is seen as the inner revolution, while Pan-Africanism is the outer revolution. The first rebuilds the mind; the second rebuilds the world.

For many African Americans, the interplay between these two philosophies reflects a deeper internal conflict: the search for

62

identity and belonging. Centuries of enslavement, segregation, and systemic racism have fractured the sense of cultural continuity that other ethnic groups may possess. The enforced adoption of European names, languages, and religions—alongside the erasure of African customs—has resulted in a "psychic exile," a sense of cultural homelessness. (Fanon & Frantz, 1952).

Afrocentricity offers a way out of this exile by inviting African Americans to rediscover their spiritual and cultural inheritance. It encourages them to see themselves not as a minority in America, but as descendants of rich African civilizations. Exploring ancient Kemet, Yoruba cosmology, or the philosophical wisdom of Ubuntu ("I am because we are") helps anchor self-identity in origins rather than oppression, transforming trauma into triumph.

However, the journey of reclamation can be complex. The African American experience is uniquely hybrid, shaped by African ancestry, American birth, and generations of resistance. The idea of "returning to Africa" is not just geographical but psychological and spiritual. The challenge lies in reconciling African heritage with American reality, as many may feel disconnected from contemporary African struggles or alienated from an identity they were encouraged to forget.

Pan-Africanism seeks to bridge this gap by reminding African Americans that their liberation is intertwined with the global condition of all African people. The advancement of any community, whether in Johannesburg, Kingston, or Chicago, uplifts the collective destiny. (Kania et al., 2011) However, achieving Pan-African unity has historically been complicated by class differences, colonial boundaries, and the lingering effects of Western influence, which may divide Africans from African Americans and even Africans from one another.

The modern challenge for African Americans, and, indeed, for the entire African diaspora, is to integrate Afrocentric consciousness with Pan-African purpose. Self-knowledge without global solidarity can become limited, while political unity without cultural grounding risks being superficial. Both philosophies must coexist: Afrocentricity grounds individual identity, while Pan-Africanism extends that identity to a global mission.

In the 21st century, African Americans stand at a crossroads between history and destiny. While technology and travel have brought the world closer together, internal divisions persist. The task is not only to reclaim the African mind but also to use it as a bridge, restoring a circle that was broken by enslavement.

Informed sociopathy

Historically, white hegemony in the United States has resulted in the systematic marginalization of African Americans through a succession of entrenched practices and institutions. These ranged from the era of slavery, through the imposition of Jim Crow laws and segregation, to the persistence of inequities in housing, education, and the legal system. (Atlanta Compromise, 2025) Tactics such as lynching, segregation, and economic exclusion not only caused collective hardship but were also frequently justified under notions of social order. (Cook et al., 2018). At the core of this structure was the denial of full personhood to African Americans, a foundational aspect that contributed to the establishment and maintenance of institutional hierarchies. Major societal institutions, including religion, law, science, and media, played central roles in sustaining and legitimizing these systems of control. (Black church - Wikipedia, n.d.).

White hegemony asserts its dominance through a web of institutional norms, policies, and practices that shape and restrict the experiences of Black communities. Enforced boundaries, manifested in segregation, public humiliation, and violence, became defining features across generations. Efforts to resist or reform these structures were often portrayed as threats to societal stability, while new forms of social control emerged over time. Each phase in this history illustrates how institutional practices have perpetuated disparities in rights and opportunities, making the struggle for equality an ongoing process.

If antisociality is understood as a persistent disregard for the rights and well-being of others, then systemic racial inequality stands as an enduring challenge within American society. (US workforce system restricts opportunities through racial discrimination, report says, 2024) These patterns influence critical domains such as democracy, justice, wealth distribution, and community stability, resulting in long-term hardship and social fragmentation.

White hegemony encompasses more than individual beliefs; it operates as a complex system of institutions, cultural norms, and everyday practices. Efforts to diminish its power have taken various forms, including policy reforms, cultural transformation, educational initiatives, and advocacy movements. Examples of such progress include civil rights legislation, affirmative action, and the growing recognition of diverse identities. (Civil Rights Act of 1964). Despite the persistence of structural inequalities evident in the transitions from slavery to Jim Crow and then to mass incarceration, these systems remain subject to reform and transformation as society advances. (Alexander & Michelle, 2010) Achieving widespread inclusion demands ongoing institutional change across sectors such as law, education, religion, and the economy.

Marginalized groups have played pivotal roles in driving social progress, even though they did not create the systems that oppressed them. Across a spectrum of resistance — from abolitionist efforts and civil rights activism to contemporary movements —society has been challenged to confront the gaps between democratic ideals and the realities of racial inequality. The creative and intellectual contributions of African Americans in music, spirituality, literature, and thought have influenced not only American culture but also global perspectives, reshaping traditional narratives. (African Americans and the Arts, 2024) Their advocacy and leadership have highlighted deep-seated issues within established systems, though such efforts have often required significant emotional, economic, and physical investment.

For meaningful and sustainable change, participation from both dominant and marginalized groups is essential. Lasting progress depends on raising awareness, engaging in honest dialogue, implementing institutional reforms, and ensuring equitable access to opportunities. Marginalized communities continue to demonstrate resilience and provide visionary leadership, while broader involvement enhances the potential for transformative outcomes.

White hegemony should be recognized as a historically constructed system that has shaped societal standards of value, beauty, intellect, and more. For African American families, this means continually navigating challenges related to identity and opportunity. Moving toward greater inclusion starts with recognizing that these hierarchies are not natural or fixed; they can be dismantled and reimagined.

Progress requires each generation to question prevailing norms, reclaim narratives through education and cultural expression, preserve heritage, provide accurate historical accounts, foster critical thinking, promote cooperative economic strategies, and encourage civic engagement. True transformation is achieved through collective effort to repair and restructure systems, shifting societal goals from exclusion to belonging and from control to stewardship. Every step made toward justice and self-worth contributes to the gradual reshaping of entrenched structures.

Section Four

Not yet determined

Having explored our beliefs and our roots,
Section Four: Information Not Yet Determined
welcomes us into a space of uncertainty and
inquiry. In this section, we encounter the limits
of understanding and consider how the
unknown shapes our culture, fears, and hopes.
These essays encourage us to meet ambiguity
with curiosity and courage, recognizing that
growth arises in spaces between certainty and
doubt.

The presence of darkness

Fear, privilege, and the defense of social hierarchy have profoundly influenced American institutions, and they consider the potential consequences as those hierarchies are challenged or dismantled.

For more than four centuries, foundational American institutions, including law, education, housing, and religion, were organized around the principle of white dominance. (How white supremacy became part of the nation's fabric, 2022). This arrangement was not just political but deeply psychological. It reassured many white Americans that their elevated position in the social order was not only earned but also divinely sanctioned. When this established order is questioned, individuals shaped by a legacy of privilege often respond with fear rather than curiosity.

Psychologists refer to this as a status-threat response: anxiety arising from the perception that one's group is losing its traditional rank or recognition. (Social identity threat, no.) This reaction is rooted less in outright hatred and more in the fear of losing certainty, mistaking privilege for fairness, and clinging to a worldview that once promised security. In this sense, white hegemony has functioned as a collective coping mechanism for a rapidly changing society.

The core anxiety is displacement. As demographic shifts and institutional diversification occur, some white Americans feel that established norms no longer guarantee their influence. Forces such as economic globalization and multicultural politics unsettle those who have been conditioned to associate whiteness with stability. This anxiety evolves into an imagined threat of extinction, as seen in conspiracy myths like the "Great Replacement," which alleges that people of color are plotting to erase white identity. Such narratives transform everyday demographic changes into existential battles, fueling the growth of white nationalist movements that cloak their aims in patriotic rhetoric while seeking to preserve dominance through anti-democratic means. (Hate groups in the US decline but their influence grows, report shows, 2025)

Institutions amplify these insecurities. Policies governing zoning, policing, education, and employment were established initially during periods when whiteness was central to the concept of citizenship. Even as explicit racism declines, these systemic frameworks continue to reproduce privilege quietly. Scholars refer to this phenomenon as structural racism: inequality perpetuated not by overt hatred, but by the routine operations of established systems. (Structural inequality, n.d.) For those invested in maintaining hierarchy, upholding these structures feels justified as a means of preserving "order." For those excluded, it represents the ongoing theft of opportunity. This psychological divide fuels contemporary culture wars.

Transitioning to a more pluralistic America holds the promise of releasing significant creative and economic energy. Diverse leadership enhances problem-solving, and greater inclusion strengthens democracy's moral authority on the global stage. However, redistributing power also provokes turbulence, unsettling bureaucracies, and provoking backlash among groups convinced that greater equality equates to loss. The nation could finally align its ideals with its practices, developing new civic rituals, curricula, and institutions that honor the full spectrum of its people's experiences.

Without addressing persistent radicalization, such as white nationalist and "replacement" narratives that weaponize fear into violence, everyone, including those who feel threatened, faces greater danger. Education and fair policies are essential to counteract such extremism.

Contemporary advocates of white dominance fall into two main categories. The first group, ideological movements and organizations like the Ku Klux Klan, Patriot Front, and Proud Boys, use mythic nationalism to mask racism. They glorify "Western civilization," recast equality as persecution, and attract followers through grievance-driven propaganda. Their primary danger lies not in numbers, but in the influence their rhetoric exerts on mainstream politics. The second group consists of institutional gatekeepers' segments within business, media, and academia, who resist diversity not through explicit slogans, but through inertia: legacy admissions, coded hiring practices, and selective empathy. Their subtle defense of privilege maintains the same hierarchy without outward symbols of extremism. Both approaches stem from the same psychological root: the fear that sharing power entails the loss of identity.

White hegemony cannot be sustained in an interdependent world. Dismantling requires more than accusations; it calls for profound transformation. Research indicates that cooperative engagement among diverse groups working toward common goals reduces prejudice. (Pettigrew et al., 2006) Honest historical education in schools and media can restore context without inducing shame. (This professor says teaching Black history is about joy, not shame, 2023)

Institutions that model transparency and fairness can weaken extremist recruitment by rebuilding trust. (Harper et al., 2023) For white Americans, relinquishing dominance does not mean losing dignity; instead, it offers the opportunity to reclaim a sense of shared humanity, defining worth by contribution instead of hierarchy. For communities of color, true inclusion involves not just representation but power-sharing and meaningful participation in shaping policy.

Each generation inherits both the promise and the pathology of the American Republic: the promise of freedom and the pathology of fear disguised as order. If white hegemony continues to dictate leadership, education, and belonging, the nation risks shrinking beneath its internal contradictions. Embracing pluralism as the next step in America's evolution can transform fear into faith, a faith in a democracy broad enough to include all colors, creeds, and consciences. The soul of America will not be preserved by maintaining power for one group, but by ensuring justice for all. That is the work that lies ahead.

It's not personal

There exists an invisible rhythm that governs all existence, a living law threading through stars, soil, thought, and time. This is the cause-and-effect of life, the continuum through which consciousness expresses itself in form. To understand this law is to grasp the very architecture of being to ignore it is to wander in confusion, mistaking the shadows of effect for the substance of cause. The faithful observer learns to perceive this invisible chain and, in doing so, becomes a conscious participant in creation.

Every event in the universe, whether grand or minute, follows a precise pattern: a cause gives birth to a condition, which in turn becomes the cause for the next event. Nothing happens in isolation. Every action, emotion, and idea sends ripples through the field of existence. Life is not a series of accidents; rather, it is a continuum of unfolding intent. The wise have recognized this principle since the dawn of consciousness.

The ancients referred to it as karma, philosophers called it determinism, and mystics described it as divine order. Regardless of the language, the essence remains constant: every outcome arises from something prior, and what is experienced reflects what has been allowed to exist within.

Within human experience, this law unfolds through a predictable sequence: First, the thought, which is the seed, the first cause. Then there is emotion, the energy that nourishes the seed. Then action, the movement of energy into the physical realm. After that experience, which is the harvest, the outer reflection of inner dynamics. And then belief, the imprint left behind, reinforces or alters the next thought. Finally, it all starts again with new thoughts. Repeatedly. The cycle continues.

Each link feeds the next, forming a self-sustaining loop of creation. Thought is the origin point; emotion energizes it. Action translates it into the physical world. Experience shapes outcomes, and belief shapes future thoughts. This sequence forms the engine of destiny and explains why two people may live in the same world but experience entirely different realities. What is held in mind becomes matter; what is feared, resisted, or denied is equally drawn into manifestation. The universe remains impartial, simply reflecting what consciousness impresses upon it.

Quantum physics suggests that observation influences outcome, yet spiritual philosophy has long acknowledged this: what you give attention to expands. Observation is not passive; it is an energetic command. To observe something consciously is to participate in its becoming. The faithful observer understands this and takes great care in contemplation, knowing that contemplation itself sets creation in motion. When faith and observation align, the cause-and-effect sequence becomes sacred rather than random. The inner world is the first cause; the outer world is its effect.

Over the past two centuries, many have served as living evidence of this law. Their journey from bondage to liberation, from anonymity to legacy, did not unfold through luck or chance, but through the steady practice of faith in action. Consider the choices made by Sandy and Racheal, descendants of Cato and Selina, during the oppressive era of Jim Crow, when they prioritized their children's education, often gathering them in secret by candlelight to teach the importance of reading and writing.

This decision planted seeds of intellectual empowerment that rippled through generations, enabling their descendants to find voices in leadership roles and advocacy. Their choice became a pivotal cause, with its effects expanding over time, making education a cornerstone for subsequent generations. This commitment to learning lifted the family from the confines of societal limitations, demonstrating that causality is not a cold mechanism but sacred continuity. The Family did not simply endure the world; they brought forth a new one through their consciousness.

The opposite of conscious causality is the fatal paradigm, the illusion that causes lie outside oneself. Those trapped within it live reactively, constantly chasing effects such as money, validation, religion, approval, and power. In this paradigm, individuals become subjects of the world rather than co-creators. Attempts to change results without transforming the thoughts that created them result in repeating cycles, crumbling empires, and persistent personal suffering.

When inner motives are unclear, external confusion often results. Clarified motives bring greater harmony. Creation involves both intention and receptivity: one supplies direction and purpose, while the other nurtures outcomes. Imbalance leads to rigidity or passivity; harmony supports new possibilities.

This balance has contributed to the Family legacy, with each generation demonstrating elements of motivation and care, sustaining ongoing creation. Each person is shaped by ancestry, culture, and inherited beliefs, but awareness allows change. Becoming conscious enables breaking cycles of suffering by identifying and rewriting root causes. True freedom arises from choosing new actions rather than being defined by past events—this is mastery.

Causality is a circular process: effects create new causes as awareness grows, and each generation broadens life's cycle. The family illustrates this evolution, genealogy links consciousness, and cosmic causality. Life mastery begins by recognizing one's role in shaping events. Thoughts, feelings, and actions influence outcomes, shifting perspective from passive observer to active creator. This marks an awakening beyond conventional paradigms—a soul recalling its authorship. We are co-creators. Life follows consciousness, not chance; recognizing this helps end the perception of victimhood.

Mela-nation

The story of humanity is written in the stars, yet it is read in the body. Among the many gifts bestowed upon humanity, melanin stands as one of the most profound biological substances, carrying with it the memory of the cosmos. Within my family legacy, the idea that life endures through transformation is mirrored in the function and symbolism of melanin. As sunlight gently warms the surface of one's skin, it ignites a golden halo that seems to pulse with the ancient echoes of the universe, bridging the gap between heaven and earth. Melanin is not merely a pigment; it represents a bridge that unites heaven and earth, energy and matter, creator, and creation, symbolizing sacred continuity.

Melanin is a biopolymer present in humans, animals, and microorganisms. Its functions are diverse: it absorbs ultraviolet (UV) radiation, neutralizes free radicals, regulates temperature, and converts light into biochemical energy. Melanin determines skin color and influences how the body interacts with solar and electromagnetic energy. These roles have been explored in the field of photobiology, but references to melanin appear in African cosmologies long before scientific explanations emerged. (Photoprotection and Skin Pigmentation: Melanin-Related Molecules and Some Other New Agents Obtained from Natural Sources, 2025, pp. 112-118)

In Kemet (ancient Egypt), blackness, called Kem, was honored as the primordial substance from which all life arose. The black soil of the Nile was revered for its fertility, productivity, and regenerative power. (Flooding of the Nile, n.d.) Similarly, the darkness of space was not considered a void but a source of creation. The Dogon people of Mali described the universe as originating from a "dark seed," a cosmic egg containing all potential life. (Cosmic egg - Wikipedia, n.d.)

This darkness was seen as intelligence at rest. Melanin, sometimes described as the "dark matter" of the human body, has been symbolically linked to generative principles that guide the formation of galaxies and stars. (Welsing & C., 1991) This suggests a deep connection between biology and cosmic concepts.

Melanin's unique capacity for solar energy absorption does not mark separation or superiority. All humans share a common origin, made of the same fundamental elements—carbon, hydrogen, oxygen, and iron that exist throughout the universe.

From a metaphysical viewpoint, the cosmos is understood as a dynamic interplay between light and darkness, energy and matter, visibility, and invisibility. Light reveals. Darkness conceals. Both are necessary for balance. In some traditions, melanin is seen as absorbing light and transforming energy into stability, supporting universal harmony. It reflects balance.

Biologically, melanin's role reflects these cosmic principles by balancing radiance with receptivity.

Traditional African spiritual philosophies recognized this balance, viewing individuals with higher melanin levels as embodying the creative tension between spirit and matter on a microcosmic scale. Melanin illustrates the diversity of biological adaptation, while simultaneously revealing the unity woven into nature's design. Some populations have adapted to thrive in intense sunlight, while others are suited to colder climates—each engaging with its environment in unique ways. Melanin is a living example of equilibrium, reminding us that all people participate in an ongoing exchange of energy, regardless of outward appearances.

In many African spiritual traditions, the body is seen as deeply connected to both spirit and cosmos. Within this framework, melanin is not just a biochemical substance, but something ancestral associated with memory, intuition, and rhythm. It is believed to facilitate connections between the nervous system and the auditory and vibratory dimensions of creation: sound, rhythm, and frequency. Through these channels, consciousness recognizes its unity with all existence. Practices like drumming, prayer, and the spoken word are thought to activate this resonance, with melanin in the body serving as an instrument attuned to the fundamental patterns of life, what ancient thought calls the Word or Logos.

If modern astrophysics teaches that everything began with dark matter and dark energy, African philosophy had already declared that creation begins in darkness. (Dark energy, n.d.) Melanin is the biological echo of this truth, a reminder that the darkness found in skin, soil, and the universe itself is not emptiness, but pure potential. The human story, then, is not one of division, but of divine reflection. Each shade of humanity expresses a unique note in the cosmic harmony of existence.

To speak of melanin is not to divide, but to remember. It is to acknowledge that the same intelligence that shapes galaxies, births stars, and sustains the rhythm of time resides within the human body. Those rich in melanin express a particular aspect of the universe's creative resilience, mirroring the dark, radiant core of existence. Yet all people, regardless of hue, share in this inheritance. We are all formed from the same cosmic dust and animated by the same divine breath. Melanin is both a scientific and symbolic testament that the cosmos does not reside only above us, but within us as well.

Seek and you will find

Before modern church traditions, the Gullah Geechee of the Carolina and Georgia Lowcountry practiced the phenomenon of "Seeking." When young boys and girls reached maturity, about 12 years old, their parents would require them to leave daily life to find God directly in nature. This tradition drew on West and Central African initiation rituals, in which isolation fostered spiritual growth. These customs survived enslavement, transforming the Southern wilderness into new sacred spaces. (Seeking | The Gullah Religious Tradition, 2022) So, when ancestors spoke of "going down in de wilderness to talk wit God," they carried on a deep African heritage adapted to their realities.

To "seek" meant to withdraw, sometimes for days, even weeks. The Seeker might disappear into the woods with nothing but a Bible, a song, and a heavy heart. They prayed, cried, fasted, sang, and waited. Some said they wrestled with the Spirit; others said they were waiting on their "sign." That they were connected to the omnipotence of the creator, no one could do it for you. Mama could not speak on your behalf, and the preacher couldn't speed it up. You stayed out there until something deep inside you changed. And when the change came, You Knew an awakening had come.

When the moment came, it wasn't subtle. Seekers described dreams, visions, and a peace that "comes down like cool water on a hot soul." That's when they'd head back home, ready for baptism in the river and a brand-new walk with the Lord.

The end of Seeking wasn't a quiet return; it was a celebration. When the Seeker returned, everyone knew. You could see it in the way they moved lighter, surer, like somebody who'd talked with God and lived to tell it. During the next church meeting or revival, the new believer would "tell their story," Describing the moment the Spirit met them. The elders would listen, nod, and sometimes shout a little, not because the tale was fancy, but because it was real. The community's witness sealed the conversion: "They have been changed." It was more than religion. It was belonging through transformation. You were no longer a spectator in faith; you were a full-fledged member of the spiritual tribe.

What makes Seeking so remarkable is the time and place it occurred. Enslaved Africans were denied freedom of body, yet they found a path to freedom of soul. In a world where everything was owned, land, labor, even time, seeking was one thing nobody could control. A person could step away from the expert's fields and meet God directly, no permission needed. That was a quiet revolution. While others preached obedience, our people practiced direct revelation. They didn't need an intermediary between themselves and the All in All. The message was clear: Freedom starts on the inside.

When I trace my family through history, that same Seeking spirit is right there under the surface. My fourth-generation grandparents, Cato and Selina, in bondage yet unbroken, carried some of that old wisdom prayer by moonlight, whispers of songs in fields. My third-generation grandparents, Sandy and Racheal, instructed their children by firelight during Jim Crow, turning lessons into liberation. Isaac and Dolly found faith not in fancy pulpits but in daily devotion and unshakable hope. Blanche and I built our home on discipline, dignity, and quiet faith, the modern face of Seeking in an age of noise. Each generation withdrew in its own way, through prayer, reflection, or hard work, and then returned to the world renewed and ready. Many families in the South have consistently transformed isolation into valuable insights and adversity into dedicated service.

The elders recognized elements of humor in Seeking. They'd say, "You better be careful what you pray for, cause when you start seeking, the Lord might just find you first!"

They told stories of folks who went out into the woods expecting angels and came back running from every squirrel and rustling leaf. Beneath the laughter lay a simple truth: the journey was sacred, combining fear, grace, and humility.

It Still Matters. Although few venture into the wilderness now, the core spirit of "Seeking" remains strong. Every time a person takes a break from the noise to rediscover themselves through meditation, prayer, journaling, or a long walk, they're doing what their ancestors did. They're stepping out to listen. To wrestle. To wait for the still, small voice that says, "You are seen, you are whole, you are free." In a modern world overflowing with distractions, seeking remains a radical act, choosing silence over noise, soul over spectacle, purpose over popularity. What wilderness might you step into this week? Inviting yourself to a small experiment in seeking can bridge your heritage into today's practice.

My family has had a tradition of seeking not just religious beliefs, but also truth, dignity, and freedom. This motivation has helped the family overcome challenges and achieve various accomplishments over generations. In this context, seeking is regarded as both a religious activity and a family custom that imparts the following lesson to each generation:

"When the world is noisy, find a quiet place. When it is dark, create your own light. When you gain new knowledge, help others do the same." This approach is consistent with past generations and continues the family name and tradition.

Section Five

The All in All

Emerging from the questions in Section Four, we now enter Section Five: The All in All. This concluding section interweaves legacy, resilience, and spiritual reflection. Here, we focus on integration and how lessons, questions, and discoveries inform a fuller sense of self and community. These final essays encourage reflection on connection, inviting your own story into the greater whole.

A deep bond

Within my family's legacy, each generation is sustained by the nourishment provided by those who came before. From Cato and Selina in the late 18th century through the many branches that followed, Sandy and Racheal, Dublin and Martha, Jessie and Sara Jane, Isaac and Dolly, Blanche and I, life has been supported by more than just blood ties; it has been enriched by memory, sacrifice, and faith. The endurance and wisdom of our ancestors feed the present, just as all biological life depends on consuming life to survive. Every generation draws upon the courage and perseverance of those who preceded it, transforming their struggles into the nutrients for growth and becoming. This reflection serves both as a meditation on the law of survival that governs all living things and as a tribute to our family's ongoing role in the eternal cycle of existence.

All forms of life require sustenance derived from other living beings. Whether through predation, absorption, or decomposition, existence is a continuous exchange of energy. Carnivores consume other animals; herbivores rely on living plants; decomposers break down the dead to pave the way for new life. Even plants, often considered self-sufficient, draw nourishment from the decayed remains of organisms in the soil. The soil itself is rich because it holds the memory of past life.

Thus, every act of living is inherently an act of remembrance, a reaffirmation that life is never created from nothing but is instead perpetually reborn through what has come before. This biological reality mirrors my family's lineage, where each generation, strengthened by its predecessors' endurance, draws power from the "living soil" of ancestral experience.

At a deeper level, the law of consumption reveals a divine pattern: life sustains itself through transformation. What one form relinquishes, another receives. Death is not an end, but a transference. When a tree falls, it becomes soil; when the soil feeds a seed, that seed grows into a new forest. The universe endlessly recycles its essence. In parallel, the family legacy transforms struggle into strength, bondage into resilience, and pain into wisdom. Consuming life becomes a sacred act, taking in what another has given. Each generation, whether they know it or not, partakes in this ancient practice: consuming the virtues, lessons, and laborers of their ancestors and transforming them into new expressions of dignity and living. Life survives by the sacrifice of another, and within this paradox lies the moral and spiritual balance of existence. In nature, nothing truly dies; it simply changes form and passes on.

Ancestors who endured oppression, displacement, and hardship became a spiritual and moral nourishment for those who followed. Cato and Selina's endurance under bondage laid the foundation for Sandy and Racheal's freedom. Isaac and Dolly's

90

service, and leadership nourished Blanche's and mine vision and dignity. This cycle persists, weaving a lineage of consumption that turns survival into purpose. No life exists in isolation. In nature, the lion relies on the gazelle for sustenance; the gazelle depends on the grass; the grass draws nourishment from the soil; and the decayed remains of past life enrich the soil itself. This interconnected cycle forms the very fabric that holds the universe together.

In much the same way, the story of a family is never solitary or self-contained. It is deeply entwined with the lives of neighbors, communities, and cultures and entities that have both nourished the family and been nourished by it in return. Every act of mentorship, compassion, or resilience, enacted within and beyond the family circle, is part of this universal exchange, receiving life by giving life.

To recognize that all biological life must consume other life for survival is to see a profound spiritual parallel. Every soul must also "consume" experience, embrace joy, sorrow, loss, and love, to grow and mature. Each generation must learn from the past to sustain and enrich the future. In this sense, the family legacy becomes an ecological truth, expressed in human form: its endurance is a living ecosystem of memory and meaning.

What the first generation endured becomes the moral nourishment for the next, the emotional sustenance for the one that follows, and the source of spiritual strength for those yet to come. Life consumes life, not as an act of violence, but as a sacred form of communion. To eat, to breathe, to remember, all are acts of participation in the same cosmic meal. The ancestors offered their essence so that their descendants might live more fully.

When the present generation gives love, wisdom, and truth to those who follow, it becomes part of that eternal table, contributing to the ongoing banquet of existence. In this way, family legacy is not merely a genealogy of names and dates; it is the unbroken succession of nourishment, a celebration in which each life feeds the next. Through this sacred consumption, all that has come before remains forever alive within those who inherit and embody the legacy.

The mindful eater

All life depends on consuming other living things. Eating is more than survival; it is a transfer of energy that keeps the cycle of creation and change in motion. From the biological viewpoint, the food we eat is no longer alive. The animal has ceased to breathe; the plant no longer grows. Yet the molecules of life—proteins, fats, carbohydrates, vitamins, and minerals—remain intact.

These molecules hold within them stored potential energy, the remnants of sunlight and motion, of growth and struggle. When we consume, our bodies disassemble the dead and reassemble their parts into the living: muscles, blood, cells, and thought. Life recycles itself through us. The food does not sustain us because it is alive, but because its structure still holds the memory of life. That memory, encoded in chemistry, is what we absorb and reanimate within ourselves.

Yet biology only tells part of the story. Beyond chemistry lies the energetic residue of being. Every creature, every plant, vibrates with a unique frequency signature of its existence. When it dies, that vibration does not vanish; it lingers in its tissues, in the very form we consume. To eat without awareness is to take that energy unconsciously, letting it blend chaotically with our own. But eating with gratitude and consciousness is to acknowledge that the life that was given transforms the act into a sacred exchange.

In that moment, the eater and the eaten are unified within a single field of being. The vibration of death becomes the hum of continued life.

This is why ancient traditions bless their meals, offer prayers, or practice ritual before eating. They understood that nourishment is not simply fuel; it is a communion. It reminds us that we live because something else no longer does, and that our existence is made possible by another's sacrifice. In nature, nothing truly ends. Death, stripped of its emotional weight, is merely a change of form. The atoms of the dead animal will one day nourish the soil that gives rise to new plants. Those plants, in turn, will feed other creatures, and so the cycle endures. This circular process reveals that life feeds on death not as punishment, but as a partnership. Every organism contributes its being to the ongoing evolution of existence. What dies becomes the foundation upon which something new is built. This is the cosmic economy, nothing wasted, everything transformed. When we eat, therefore, we are not consuming death but participating in rebirth. Meat, fruit, and grain are remnants of ancient sunlight and memory, woven into existence and transformed by life.

An enhanced understanding of this principle fosters mindful eating and living. It prompts us to acknowledge the fluid boundary between life and death, emphasizing that we remain intrinsically connected to what we consume and, in effect, are its extension. Each breath, each bite, each heartbeat is the universe recycling itself. To live mindfully is to honor that process, to recognize that every meal is both an ending and a beginning, a prayer made fresh.

Life feeds on death so that the song of existence never stops. In this way, nourishment is not destruction but renewal, not loss but transformation. The true mystery of eating lies not in consuming the dead, but in realizing that the dead are never truly gone. They live again, within us, as us, through us.

Transformed

From the dawn of creation, one truth has never changed: life feeds on life. It is a law written into the very bones of the universe. The living creature draws sustenance from what has passed, and in so doing, ensures that life itself never ends. My family's story, spanning from Cato and Selina in the late 1700s to the present generations, stands as a living testament to this sacred cycle. Through struggle, loss, and renewal, our family has continually transformed what was once broken into what could live again. When Cato and Selina stood at the root of this family tree, their world was defined by bondage and hardship. Yet, even within oppression, life persisted, growing in secret, feeding on faith, resilience, and the will to survive. What they endured was not wasted; it became the fertile ground from which generations would rise.

In a cosmic sense, their suffering became nutrient, transmuted through time into strength, education, artistry, and love. Just as the earth transforms decay into the life of new trees, my ancestors transformed tragedy into endurance, ensuring that the spirit of their lineage continued to breathe. Every generation after Cato and Selina, Sandy and Rachael, Dublin and Martha, Jessie and Sara Jane, Isaac and Dolly, Blanche and I, Lee, Camille, and Matthew have, in some way, fed upon the lessons of the past. This nourishment is not literal but exists in the way memory enriches consciousness.

Each child born into the family line carries the remnants of those who came before: the struggles, the laughter, the teachings, and the prayers whispered in the dark. Like the human body that rebuilds itself from the remnants of what it consumes, our family spirit continually rebuilds itself from ancestral wisdom, living proof that what dies is never gone, only transformed into the following expression of life.

Beyond the visible lineage lies an energetic inheritance, a vibration that binds the family across time. Each ancestor added a frequency to the great song of the collective family spirit. When one generation passes, its vibration does not end; it hums quietly within the hearts of the living. This is why certain traits, courage, empathy, integrity, and faith, echo through the generations. These are not accidents, but vibrational inheritances: the unseen life-force sustaining the family long after physical death. To eat, to breathe, to live consciously within that vibration is to honor those who came before and to ensure that their energy and sacrifices continue to nourish the living.

In a broader sense, my family's legacy reflects the same cosmic pattern that governs nature: transformation through exchange. The ancestors gave their lives, labor, and faith, and from that offering came new life, understanding, and purpose. Their hardships were passed down and metabolized into wisdom. Their silence became the language of persistence. Their tears became the rivers of compassion still flowing through the family's heart. Remembering them is to partake of their essence, not as ghosts of the past, but as living sustenance for the soul of today.

From Cato's unyielding spirit in bondage to the creativity and leadership of his descendants in freedom, the family's history mirrors the law of the cosmos: life feeds on death so that love, wisdom, and purpose may endure. Just as the body transforms food into energy, the family transforms history into strength. Each generation carries the previous one forward, not merely as memory, but as living matter, mind, and soul. To live is to understand that death does not end life; it renews it. Each ancestor, in giving of themselves, ensured the vitality of those yet unborn. Every triumph, every lesson, every sacrifice became nourishment for the next generation.

What dies feeds what lives. What was lost gives rise to what is found. And through this sacred exchange, life never ends; it simply changes form. In every breath of the present generation and the newest family members, the pulse of Cato and Selina still beats. Their essence, transmuted through the centuries, remains the invisible sustenance that keeps the family name alive.

Iron sharpens iron

Every family's got a story, but the Dingle story could fill volumes, history, drama, faith, heartbreak, and a good dose of humor to wash it all down. Spanning generations, from Cato and Selina in the late 1700s through Sandy and Racheal, Dublin and Martha, Jessie and Sara Jane, Isaac and Dolly, Blanche and I, to Lee, Camille, and the latest branches, London, Autumn, and Levi, the Dingles have accomplished what many thought impossible: survive, rise, and keep their laughter intact.

What began in the fields of bondage grew into a forest of faith and resilience. Each generation carried the memory of struggle like a seed in its pocket, planting it wherever they found ground. From that seed sprouted strength, dignity, and a legacy that continues to bloom. The Dingles bore burdens no one should have to endure enslavement, displacement, segregation, and redlining, each era adding another brick to the load.

Trauma did not just live in history books; it became embedded in their very being. The effects of these hardships are still visible: a cautious hesitation when opportunity arises, or the need to work twice as hard to feel "good enough." These are remnants of centuries spent striving to prove an inherent worth. When the past was stolen, names, languages, and stories were left silent where memory should have been, making it difficult to see clearly.

Generations of Dingles walked through this identity fog, yet they did not succumb to self-pity. Instead, they transformed pain into power and built something solid from the ashes, with each generation contributing a new chapter to the family's ongoing narrative.

Sandy and Racheal educated children in the shadow of Jim Crow laws. Isaac managed government operations with fairness rooted in ancestral discipline. Dolly created a sanctuary at home, her kitchen serving as both prayer room and command center. Blanche and I established a household centered on education, hard work, and love. The present generation carries the torch, turning survival into artistry, entrepreneurship, and legacy. The Dingles did not just survive history; they outsmarted it. Trauma leaves marks, but resilience builds calluses that become tools for forging ahead. What was once vigilance for danger evolved into an awareness of opportunity. Suspicion became discernment; necessity-bred work ethic became intentional excellence. Faith, once an imposed shackle, became a key to freedom.

The Dingles learned that faith is more than kneeling on Sunday; it is the daily act of rising again on Monday. This is the heart of "the faithful observer": seeing the world as it is, while steadfastly believing in what it can become. Yet, amid these triumphs, the persistence of inequities reminds us of the ongoing striving for justice and equality. This unyielding journey continues to shape the family's narrative, illustrating both resilience and the enduring push for progress.

Having endured centuries of loss, the Dingles mastered the art of giving back. They understood the importance of balance, knowing that land could heal if respected, communities could thrive through generosity, and love multiplied when shared. Those who have turned brokenness into beauty are uniquely qualified to help heal the world. Through gardens, mentorship, education, or simply showing up, the family has always worked to brighten their corner of the world and make the earth a kinder place.

It is essential to stay grounded and not romanticize suffering. No one seeks wisdom through pain, and if trauma were a family business, it would be best shut down. Yet, the Dingle way is to find laughter in the storm and humor amidst the mess, sustaining the spirit. A Sunday dinner filled with love, side-eye, and sweet tea can heal more than most sermons. True healing means learning to laugh without guilt, rest without apology, and dream freely. It is about teaching the next generation that strength includes gentleness and the wisdom to be soft when needed.

The Dingle legacy demonstrates that no darkness can extinguish a light that remembers its source. From Cato and Selina's resilience to the creative fire of London, Autumn, and Levi, the family has passed down more than names: a distinct way of seeing the world. Even when roots are buried in pain, the branches reach for the light, embodying the quiet faith that life's harshest blows can be transformed into instruments of grace. We simply did not survive history; we rewrote it, leaving behind a message for every future generation: turn what breaks you into what builds you. Keep your laughter loud, your roots deep, and your faith broad enough to embrace the world. This essay honors all Dingles across generations who chose love over resentment, meaning over self-pity, and legacy over loss. Their story is proof that, regardless of beginnings, we were never meant to end in brokenness. We are the dream our ancestors prayed for, and we are still rising.

To the readers, I invite you to reflect on your family's journey. Share your stories of resilience and triumph, celebrating the moments that shaped you and those who came before. By doing so, we honor not only our past but also the collective strength that connects us all. Your family's legacy, just like mine, can serve as an inspiration for future generations to rise and rewrite their histories. As a tangible next step, I encourage you to record one ancestor's story before the weekend. This small action can transform reflection into a meaningful contribution to your family's legacy.

Deeper Still

Let's step back and look at what this journey has uncovered: the way we see the universe, the troubles that can arise in society, and the habits we inherit all work together to shape how we live and what we believe. In plain terms, our stories about where we come from help us understand our place in the world; the rules and traditions we inherit can sometimes cause harm if they become rigid or unjust; and the patterns we learn are often passed down, quietly shaping how we act and think. When we put these ideas together, we get a clearer picture of how people make sense of their lives and why they behave the way they do.

Cosmology is just the big story a culture talks about the universe, our purpose, and how everything fits together. When these stories line up with what feels authentic and balanced, they bring meaning and peace. But if they're out of sync with reality or become twisted, we can end up feeling lost or split inside. Sometimes, I wrestle with this myself, torn between the deep roots of African tradition and the pressures of Western thinking. I ask myself: How do I honor my ancestors without losing myself in someone else's story? It's a real, ongoing tensional push-and-pull between diverse ways of seeing the world. That struggle often leads to confusion, but it also opens space for growth.

Problems start when the rules and institutions of a society, grounded in broken or harmful worldviews, become tools for keeping people down rather than lifting them. For instance, in the United States, white cultural dominance has influenced laws, churches, and schools, frequently forcing Black communities and other groups to strive for recognition and representation. Sometimes, pushing back against these systems leads to resistance and change, but at other times, people go along to get by, even when it means swallowing ideas that don't serve them.

There have been times in American history when some folks in marginalized communities tried to fit in, even if it meant accepting ideas or rules that weren't fair. But repeatedly, African Americans have found ways to turn challenging situations into chances to stand up for what's right, reshaping faith, dignity, and truth to claim their own power and build strength together.

Make it, makes sense.

People are shaped by media, religion, education, and politics to conform and react emotionally, commercially, and politically in ways that uphold existing power structures. In this way, conditioning makes social pathology appear "normal." True liberation begins only when individuals awaken, question inherited norms and reclaim their cosmological identity. Put simply, if people forget or lose their own cosmology, they may end up living according to someone else's harmful beliefs.

Healing demands deconditioning the mind, restoring a healthy cosmological foundation, and rebuilding social norms that reflect balance, justice, and collective humanity. Societies are not shaped solely by their laws or leaders; instead, they are deeply influenced by the invisible force of conditioning. These are the subtle, repetitive influences that teach individuals how to think, what to value, and whom to follow. From the very beginning of life, people are woven into intricate patterns of belief through the combined influence of family, media, religion, education, and politics. These interconnected systems work together to create a collective script—one that rewards those who conform and discourages anyone who dares to deviate.

Over time, the ways we're taught to think and act can quietly become part of us, even when we don't notice it. We pick up habits and ideas from family, media, and culture, and often take them for granted, thinking they're just how things are. But absolute freedom comes when we pause and ask: Are these beliefs really mine, or am I just playing a role I was handed? By looking at the big picture, how worldviews, social problems, and conditioning all work together, we can start to see what's really shaping us. That's when we can choose what matters and defines who we are, both as individuals and as a community.

I hope that this work gets you thinking about your own roots, not just where you come from in the universe, but what gives your life meaning. In the end, these questions about where we belong and why we're here shape everything about how we live and connect. Which inherited script are you ready to rewrite today?

When a person understands their true origins, they find their proper place within the grand design of existence. Life then becomes an extension of a sacred order. In the absence of this foundational understanding, the sense of self becomes lost, uncertain of both its purpose and its beginnings. Therefore, the pursuit of self-identity is, at its core, a cosmological journey, a return to alignment with the universe that gave birth to us and with the ancestral truths that infuse our lives with meaning. Sometimes there are more questions than answers: Who are you? Where are you from? And what are you representing on this planet?

Journeyings

This book is a map of how my family and yours have survived, adapted, and grown, both spiritually and emotionally. Our story begins with our ancestor, who faced the harsh realities of life but found a way to awaken to self-realization. From the past to the present, each generation of our collective family has learned to balance the demands of the Western world with the deep, soulful memory of our roots. As we close this collection, let us hold onto the legacy of resilience and unity: "We are the bridge our ancestors dreamed of being."

Spiritually, our journey is one of transformation. What started as an imposed Western theology became a source of hidden strength and liberation. In the Carolina Lowcountry, ancestors turned sermons into symbols and hymns into secret messages. The Christian God became not a distant figure, but a familiar, responsive presence, one that echoed the rhythms and unity of Africa. Through spiritual practices such as "seeking," they fused African and Western faiths, finding meaning in rivers, songs, and prayers. They learned to walk two paths: one for survival, and one for staying true to their origins.

Emotionally, families mastered the art of turning pain into poetry. In a world where showing true feelings could be dangerous, they learned to express themselves through coded emotions, a smile to hide sorrow, laughter to carry courage, and songs to ease fatigue. Love, humor, and empathy became the medicine that helped us endure. Over time, this emotional intelligence grew into a quiet spiritual technology, transforming hurt into harmony and sorrow into survival.

Mentally, we learned to think strategically and value education, not just as a means of survival, but to honor our ancestors and prepare for the future. Formal schooling was necessary, but so was the wisdom passed down through stories, observation, and connection to nature. We learned to speak the language of the West, but our thoughts still danced to the rhythm of Africa.

Physically, our bodies became living proof of resilience. From the fields to the factories, churches, and schools, every movement was an act of resistance and dignity. Dance, dress, and ritual helped us reclaim our sense of self, even when the world tried to commodify Black bodies. Through it all, we carried the spark of divinity within us.

At the heart of our story is an Afrocentric worldview: the belief that everything is connected, that ancestors are always near, and that a balance between the seen and the unseen is essential. Even as we navigated Western institutions, we held onto the African cosmology of wholeness: family as community, land as living memory, and God as vibration and voice. This allowed us to survive without surrendering, to adapt without losing ourselves, and to blend tradition with innovation.

The story of African Americans is not just about endurance; it's about transformation. We've turned suffering into strength, dislocation into direction, and memory into meaning. Survival is more than staying alive; it's a spiritual act, a declaration of purpose, and a covenant with those who came before. We harmonize faith with reason, culture with circumstance, and history with hope. In reclaiming our story, we reclaim ourselves. Our legacy proves that even when history tried to divide our bodies from our spirits, the spirit never forgot its way home and strengthened intergenerational bonds. By analyzing the mechanisms through which families transmit heritage and meaning, this volume advances the argument that the active cultivation of legacy is instrumental in shaping both personal and collective futures.

Summary

The Dingle Family Legacy Project stands at the intersection of history, psychology, cosmology, and cultural survival. At its core, the project investigates how a person, severed from their original cosmologies, forced into an alien cultural framework, and subjected to generations of trauma, managed not merely to endure, but to reconstruct meaning.

The project rests on four primary pillars:

The essays recognize cosmology, the story we tell about how the universe works, as the root of personal and collective identity. The Dingle family journey illustrates how African cosmological principles continued underground, beneath Christian doctrine and Western conditioning, shaping intuition, inner knowing, gender balance, and generational resilience.

Through enslavement, segregation, migration, and systemic pressure, the Dingle legacy demonstrates how trauma alters the psyche—and how adaptation becomes both a survival strategy and self-reclamation. The family's story becomes a case study in *transgenerational psychological evolution*.

The project explores the tension between religious faith (external authority) and inner knowingness (internal authority). It weaves in quantum concepts—not as physics, but as metaphors for consciousness and intention. The Dingle story shows how the locus of power gradually shifted inward across generations.

The work dissects how cultural norms shape perceptions of self and community, particularly in America, where racial hierarchies and social pathology distort both identity and possibility. The Dingle narrative reveals how families find freedom not by rejecting society, but by understanding its mechanisms and reclaiming agency.

Taken together, the project describes a 200-year evolution of consciousness within one family and, by extension, within people. It is history, but also philosophy. It is genealogy, but also cosmology. It is memory, but also transformation.

In the quiet moments, when the tide is low and the creeks of Sullivan's Island breathe their ancient rhythm, I often think about how far we've come not just as a family, but as a consciousness. Cato did not know the language of cosmology. Selina did not speak of quantum observation. Sandy never used the word ontology. Dublin did not debate the nature of faith. And yet, *they lived through these truths*. They practiced inner knowing long before there was a name for it. They trusted the unseen long before science confirmed observation's power. They carried African cosmology in instinct, intuition, rhythm, and resilience, even as they were forced to speak the language of Western doctrine.

111

Each generation moved the thread forward: from survival to self-definition, from obedience to understanding, from external authority to inner authority, from trauma to transformation. I am simply the one who stopped long enough to notice the pattern. My life, like theirs, was shaped by forces I could not immediately see. Military discipline, public service, spiritual searching, philosophical inquiry, ancestral calling. Slowly, I came to understand that my story was the continuation of a much older story.

The Dingle legacy is not about what we endured. It is about what we *carried through* endurance. It is about how we remembered, even when our memories were taken. How we rose, even when rising seemed impossible. How we maintained dignity in a world that sought to take it away. How we rediscovered our cosmology across centuries of erasure. This book is not an ending. It is the beginning. A new chapter for those who follow, for London, Autumn, Levi, and all who will stand at the edge of the same creeks asking, *"Who am I?"*

May this work be their compass. May it ground them, guide them, and challenge them. May it help them see that they are not simply descendants, they are continuations. The thread is unbroken. The story is still unfolding. And now, finally, it has been named.

Reference Lists

(n.d.). Crossroads (folklore).
en.wikipedia.org/wiki/Crossroads_(folklore).
https://en.wikipedia.org/wiki/Crossroads_(folklore)

(n.d.). Hoodoo (spirituality). Wikipedia.
https://en.wikipedia.org/wiki/Hoodoo_%28spirituality%29

(2022). Seeking | The Gullah Religious Tradition.
lowcountrygullah.com. https://lowcountrygullah.com/seeking-
the-gullah-religious-tradition/

Okun & Tema. (1999). White Supremacy Culture.
https://en.wikipedia.org/wiki/White_Supremacy_Culture

(n.d.). African Americans and Education During Reconstruction:
The Tolson's Chapel Schools. National Park Service.
https://www.nps.gov/articles/African-Americans-and-
Education-during-reconstruction-the-tolson-s-chapel-
schools.htm

(1963). Letter from Birmingham Jail.
https://en.wikipedia.org/wiki/Letter_from_Birmingham_Jail

(2025). Harriet Tubman Quotes: Six Sayings to Celebrate an Abolitionist On the 105th Anniversary of Her Death. Newsweek. https://www.newsweek.com/harriet-tubman-quotes-105th-anniversary-slavery-history-839450

(n.d.). Rosa Parks quote: I would like to be remembered as a person who.... www.azquotes.com/quote/225376. https://www.azquotes.com/quote/225376

Baldwin & James. (1962). As Much Truth as One Can Bear. The New York Times Book Review. https://www.nytimes.com/1962/01/14/archives/as-much-truth-as-one-can-bear-to-speak-out-about-the-world-as-it-is.html

(n.d.). Red pill and blue pill. en.wikipedia.org/wiki/Red_pill_and_blue_pill. https://en.wikipedia.org/wiki/Red_pill_and_blue_pill

(n.d.). Mojo bag. en.wikipedia.org/wiki/Mojo bag. https://en.wikipedia.org/wiki/Mojo_bag

(1903). The Souls of Black Folk. The Souls of Black Folk. https://en.wikipedia.org/wiki/The_Souls_of_Black_Folk

(n.d.). Ubuntu philosophy. en.wikipedia.org/wiki/Ubuntu philosophy. https://en.wikipedia.org/wiki/Ubuntu_philosophy

(n.d.). Hoodoo (spirituality).
en.wikipedia.org/wiki/Hoodoo_%28spirituality%29.
https://en.wikipedia.org/wiki/Hoodoo_%28spirituality%29

(n.d.). Maat. Encyclopedia Britannica.
https://www.britannica.com/topic/Maat-Egyptian-goddess

(n.d.). Ubuntu philosophy. en.wikipedia.org/wiki/Ubuntu
philosophy. https://en.wikipedia.org/wiki/Ubuntu_philosophy

(2008). Ifa is a divination system. UNESCO Intangible Cultural
Heritage. https://ich.unesco.org/en/RL/00146

Bois, D. & W.E.B. (1903). The Souls of Black Folk. The Souls of
Black Folk. New York: Avenel, NJ: Gramercy Books; 1994.
https://en.wikipedia.org/wiki/The_Souls_of_Black_Folk

(n.d.). Frantz Fanon – Roots and Narcissism.
frontiertherapymagazine.com.
https://frontiertherapymagazine.com/2015/03/09/118/

Asante & Kete, M. (1980). Afrocentricity: The Theory of Social
Change. Temple University Press.
https://www.amazon.com/Afrocentricity-Theory-Social-
Change/dp/0913543530

Muasya & Njeri, J. (2020). Decolonizing Religious Education to Enhance Sustainable Development in Africa: Evidence from Literature. East African Journal of Education Studies 3. https://journals.eanso.org/index.php/eajes/article/view/320

(2023). Colonial Legacies: Slavery, Christianity, and the Transformation of Indigenous Liberian Religious-Cultural Identities. https://rsisinternational.org/journals/ijrias/articles/colonial-legacies-slavery-christianity-and-the-transformation-of-indigenous-liberian-religious-cultural-identities/

(n.d.). The Bible was used to justify slavery. Then Africans made Christianity their path to freedom. www.washingtonpost.com/local/the-bible-was-used-to-justify-slavery-then-africans-made-it-their-path-to-freedom/2019/04/29/34699e8e-6512-11e9-82ba-fcfeff232e8f_story.html. https://www.washingtonpost.com/local/the-bible-was-used-to-justify-slavery-then-africans-made-it-their-path-to-freedom/2019/04/29/34699e8e-6512-11e9-82ba-fcfeff232e8f_story.html.

(n.d.). African Methodist Episcopal Church. en.wikipedia.org/wiki/African_Methodist_Episcopal_Church. https://en.wikipedia.org/wiki/African_Methodist_Episcopal_Church

(n.d.). Dotawo. Wikipedia: Dotawo.
https://en.wikipedia.org/wiki/Dotawo

(2023). Movements, Motions, Moments: Photographs of
Religion and Spirituality from the National Museum of African
American History and Culture. National Museum of African
American History and Culture.
https://nmaahc.si.edu/about/news/national-museum-African-
American-History-and-Culture-Releases-book-Black-Religion

(2023). Sacred Trees & Spirit Forests: Nature in African Spiritual
Cosmology. tropiki.no. https://tropiki.no/en_gb/african-sacred-
trees-spirit-forests

(n.d.). Songs of the Underground Railroad.
en.wikipedia.org/wiki/Songs_of_the_Underground_Railroad.
https://en.wikipedia.org/wiki/Songs_of_the_Underground_Rai
lroad

(n.d.). Juneteenth and the Black Church. Unity.org.
https://www.unity.org/en/article/juneteenth-and-black-church

(n.d.). The Historic Legacy of Black Charleston Church Where
the Shooting Occurred. Time.
https://time.com/3926257/charleston-church-emanuel-african-
methodist/

King & Jr., M. L. (1963). Strength to Love. Harper & Row. https://en.wikipedia.org/wiki/Strength_to_Love

Gamboa & Isaias. (2012). We Shall Overcome: Sacred Song on the Devil's Tongue. Amapola Publishers. https://en.wikipedia.org/wiki/We_Shall_Overcome%3A_Sacred_Song_on_the_Devil%27s_Tongue

Harrell & P., S. (2022). Rising Rooted: Black Wisdom as Emancipatory Contemplative Practice for Resilience, Healing, and Liberation. Journal of Contemplative Inquiry 9. https://digscholarship.unco.edu/joci/vol9/iss1/9

Asante & Kete, M. (1980). Afrocentricity: The Theory of Social Change. Temple University Press. https://www.amazon.com/Afrocentricity-Theory-Social-Change/dp/0915923030

(n.d.). Pan-Africanism. en.wikipedia.org/wiki/Pan-Africanism. https://en.wikipedia.org/wiki/Pan-Africanism

(n.d.). Pan-Africanism - Wikipedia. en.wikipedia.org/wiki/Pan-Africanism. https://en.wikipedia.org/wiki/Pan-Africanism

Fanon & Frantz. (1952). Black Skin, White Masks. Éditions du Seuil.
https://en.wikipedia.org/wiki/Black_Skin%2C_White_Masks

Kania, John, Kramer & Mark. (2011). Collective Impact. Stanford Social Innovation Review 9.
https://ssir.org/articles/entry/collective_impact

(2025). Atlanta Compromise. en.wikipedia.org/wiki/Atlanta Compromise.
https://en.wikipedia.org/wiki/Atlanta_Compromise

Cook, D. L., Logan, D. T., Parman, & M. J. (2018). Racial Segregation and Southern Lynching. Social Science History 42.
https://www.cambridge.org/core/journals/social-science-history/article/racial-segregation-and-southern-lynching/970ED0F6524CEDD6A9AFC2BA82A5AADB

(n.d.). Black church - Wikipedia. en.wikipedia.org/wiki/Black church. https://en.wikipedia.org/wiki/Black_church

(2024). The US workforce system restricts opportunities through racial discrimination, a report says. Joint Center for Political and Economic Studies.
https://www.reuters.com/sustainability/society-equity/us-workforce-system-restricts-opportunities-through-racial-discrimination-report-2024-09-23/

(1964). Civil Rights Act of 1964. U.S. Government Printing Office. https://www.govinfo.gov/content/pkg/STATUTE-78/pdf/STATUTE-78-Pg241.pdf

Alexander & Michelle. (2010). The New Jim Crow: Mass Incarceration in the Age of Colorblindness. The New Press. https://en.wikipedia.org/wiki/The_New_Jim_Crow

(2024). African Americans and the Arts. Association for the Study of African American Life and History. https://asalh.org/wp-content/uploads/2023/11/2024-Black-History-Theme-African-Americans-and-the-Arts.pdf

(2022). How white supremacy became part of the nation's fabric. https://news.harvard.edu/gazette/story/2022/09/how-nations-schools-taught-white-supremacism/

(n.d.). Social identity threat. en.wikipedia.org/wiki/Social_identity_threat. https://en.wikipedia.org/wiki/Social_identity_threat

(2025). Hate groups in the US decline, but their influence grows, report shows. Southern Poverty Law Center. https://apnews.com/article/e84bab8092fc15a0425a58f5ebb0cc
23

(n.d.). Structural inequality. en.wikipedia.org/wiki/Structural inequality. https://en.wikipedia.org/wiki/Structural_inequality

Pettigrew, F. T., Tropp, R. L. (2006). A Meta-Analytic Test of Intergroup Contact Theory. Psychological Science 17. https://pubmed.ncbi.nlm.nih.gov/16649810/

(2023). This professor says teaching Black history is about joy, not shame. WUSF Public Media. https://www.wusf.org/education/2023-02-20/professor-teaching-black-history-about-joy-not-shame

Harper, B. S., Weber, & S. E. (2023). Fiduciary Responsibility: Facilitating Public Trust in Automated Decision Making. https://arxiv.org/abs/2301.10001

(2025). Photoprotection and Skin Pigmentation: Melanin-Related Molecules and Some Other New Agents Obtained from Natural Sources. Journal of Photochemistry and Photobiology B: Biology 220, pp. 112-118. https://pubmed.ncbi.nlm.nih.gov/32230973/

(n.d.). Flooding of the Nile. en.wikipedia.org/wiki/Flooding_of_the_Nile. https://en.wikipedia.org/wiki/Flooding_of_the_Nile

(n.d.). Cosmic egg - Wikipedia.
en.wikipedia.org/wiki/Cosmic_egg.
https://en.wikipedia.org/wiki/Cosmic_egg

Welsing & C., F. (1991). The Isis Papers: The Keys to the Colors.
Third World Press.
https://en.wikipedia.org/wiki/The_Isis_Papers%3A_The_Keys
_to_the_Colors

(n.d.). Dark energy. en.wikipedia.org.
https://en.wikipedia.org/wiki/Dark_energy

(2022). Seeking | The Gullah Religious Tradition.
https://lowcountrygullah.com/seeking-the-gullah-religious-
tradition

Made in the USA
Columbia, SC
20 January 2026

77792254R00080